# CONTENTS

## PART ONE
### INTRODUCTION

Study and revision advice ............................................................. 5

## PART TWO
### THE POEMS

John Donne: 'The Sun Rising' ........................................................ 6
Christopher Marlowe: 'The Passionate Shepherd to His Love' ................ 8
Christina Rossetti: 'Cousin Kate' ................................................... 9
William Shakespeare: 'Sonnet 18' .................................................. 10
Elizabeth Barrett Browning: 'Sonnet 43' ......................................... 11
Carol Ann Duffy: 'Valentine' ........................................................ 12
Robert Graves: 'A Frosty Night' .................................................... 14
John Donne: 'The Flea' ............................................................... 15
John Donne: 'Holy Sonnet 17' ...................................................... 16
Tony Harrison: 'Long Distance II' .................................................. 17
Gillian Clarke: 'Catrin' ............................................................... 18
Seamus Heaney: 'Follower' .......................................................... 19
Charles Causley: 'What Has Happened to Lulu?' ............................... 20
Seamus Heaney: 'Mid-Term Break' ................................................ 21
Jon Stallworthy: 'The Almond Tree' ............................................... 22
Louis MacNeice: 'Prayer Before Birth' ............................................ 24
Ben Jonson: 'On My First Son' ..................................................... 25
Elizabeth Jennings: 'My Grandmother' ........................................... 26
Caroline Norton: 'My Heart is Like a Withered Nut!' .......................... 27
Ted Hughes: 'Old Age Gets Up' .................................................... 28
Sheenagh Pugh: 'Sweet 18' ......................................................... 29
Dylan Thomas: 'Do Not Go Gentle Into That Good Night' .................... 30
William Shakespeare: 'Crabbed Age and Youth' ................................ 31
Robert Browning: 'Porphyria's Lover' ............................................. 32
Dylan Thomas: 'I Have Longed to Move Away' .................................. 34
W. H. Davies: 'Leisure' ............................................................... 35
Carol Ann Duffy: 'Human Interest' ................................................ 36
Ted Hughes: 'Hawk Roosting' ...................................................... 37
Robert Browning: 'My Last Duchess' .............................................. 38
Percy Bysshe Shelley: 'Ozymandias' .............................................. 39
Edwin Muir: 'The Interrogation' .................................................... 40
Vernon Scannell: 'They Did Not Expect This' ................................... 41
Louis MacNeice: 'Meeting Point' ................................................... 42
Philip Larkin: 'Afternoons' ........................................................... 44
Carol Ann Duffy: 'Havisham' ........................................................ 45
Robert Herrick: 'To the Virgins, To Make Much of Time' ..................... 46
Aphra Behn: Song: 'The Willing Mistriss' ........................................ 47
Andrew Marvell: 'To His Coy Mistress' ........................................... 48
Christina Walsh: 'A Woman to Her Lover' ........................................ 50
Seamus Heaney: 'Twice Shy' ........................................................ 51
William King: 'The Beggar Woman' ................................................ 52
Sir Thomas Wyatt: 'Whoso List to Hunt' ......................................... 53
William Shakespeare: 'Sonnet 116' ................................................ 54
William Shakespeare: 'Sonnet 130' ................................................ 55
Alice Gray Jones: 'Song of the Worker's Wife' .................................. 56

## PART TWO
### The Poems

Katherine Philips: 'A Married State' ................................................ 57
R. S. Thomas: 'Chapel Deacon' ...................................................... 58
Dylan Thomas: 'The Hunchback in the Park' .................................. 59
D. J. Enright: 'Displaced Person Looks at a Cage-bird' .................... 60
Siegfried Sassoon: 'Base Details' ................................................... 61
Sheenagh Pugh: 'The Capon Clerk' ............................................... 62
U. A. Fanthorpe: 'You Will Be Hearing From Us Shortly' ................ 63
W. H. Auden: 'Refugee Blues' ....................................................... 64
Thomas Hardy: 'In Church' ........................................................... 66
Wilfred Owen: 'Dulce et Decorum Est' .......................................... 67
Dylan Thomas: 'A Refusal To Mourn the Death, by Fire, of a Child in London' .... 68
Rupert Brooke: 'The Soldier' ......................................................... 69
Wilfrid Gibson: 'The Conscript' ..................................................... 70
Philip Larkin: 'MCMXIV' ............................................................... 71
Alfred Lord Tennyson: 'The Charge of the Light Brigade' .............. 72
Wilfred Owen: 'The Send-Off' ....................................................... 74
Thomas Hardy: 'The Man He Killed' .............................................. 75
Thomas Hardy: 'Drummer Hodge' ................................................ 76
Siegfried Sassoon: 'The Hero' ....................................................... 77
Progress and revision check............................................................ 78

## PART THREE
### Key Themes

Key themes................................................................................... 79
Progress and revision check............................................................ 86

## PART FOUR
### Language and Structure

Language....................................................................................... 87
Structure....................................................................................... 89
Progress and revision check............................................................ 90

## PART FIVE
### Grade Booster

Understanding the task .................................................................. 91
Planning your answer..................................................................... 92
How to use quotations .................................................................. 93
Linking Shakespeare and poetry..................................................... 94
Sitting the controlled assessment .................................................. 96
Improve your grade ...................................................................... 97
Annotated sample answers ........................................................... 98
Further controlled assessment-style tasks ...................................... 102

Literary terms............................................................................... 102
Checkpoint answers ...................................................................... 104

## Study and revision advice

There are two main stages to your reading and work on the *WJEC Poetry Collection*. Firstly, the study of the poems as you read them. Secondly, your preparation or revision for the controlled assessment. These top tips will help you with both.

 **READING AND STUDYING THE POEMS – DEVELOP INDEPENDENCE!**

- Try to engage and respond **personally** to the ideas and stories – not just for your enjoyment, but also because it helps you develop your own, **alternative responses and thoughts** about the poems. This is something that examiners are very keen to see.

- **Talk** about the poems with friends and family; ask questions in class; put forward your own viewpoint – and, if time, **read around** the poems to find out about the context and how the poems and poets link together.

- Take time to **consider** and **reflect** about the **key elements** of the poems you are studying; keep your own notes, mind-maps, diagrams, scribbled jottings about the poems and how you respond to them; follow the structure of each poem as it progresses (what do you think might happen?); discuss the main themes and ideas that interested the poet (how does it link to the theme you are studying? Does it tackle several themes?); pick out language that impresses you or makes an **impact**, and so on.

- Treat your studying **creatively**. When you write essays or give talks about the poems make your responses creative. Think about using really clear and confident ways of explaining yourself, use unusual but apt **quotations**, well-chosen **vocabulary**, and try powerful, persuasive ways of beginning or ending what you say or write.

**EXAMINER'S TIP**

Prepare for the assessment! Whatever you need to bring, make sure you have it with you – books, if you're allowed, pens, pencils – and that you turn up on time!

 **REVISION – DEVELOP ROUTINES AND PLANS!**

- **Good revision** and **preparation** for the **controlled assessment** comes from **good planning**. Find out when the assessment begins and then plan to look at key poems on different days or times during your preparation period. You could use these Notes – see **How can these Notes help me?** – and add dates or times when you are going to cover a particular topic, poem or link to your Shakespeare play.

- Use **different ways** of **revising**. Sometimes talking about the poems and what you know/don't know with a friend or member of the family can help; at other times, filling a sheet of A4 with all your ideas in different coloured pens about a particular poem, for example 'Sweet 18', can make ideas come alive; or you could make short lists of quotations to learn, or number events in the poem to assist you.

- **Practise plans** and **essays**. As you get nearer the assessment time, start by looking at task **questions** and write short bulleted plans. Do several plans (you don't have to write the whole essay); then take those plans and add details to them (quotations, linked ideas). Finally, using the advice in **Part Five: Grade Booster**, write some practice essays and then check them out against the advice we have provided.

## John Donne: 'The Sun Rising'

### SUMMARY

① The speaker scolds the sun for waking him and his lover. Lovers, he says, are not governed by time, and he tells the sun to bother those who do need to worry about it.

② The speaker claims that he can blot out the sun with a wink, but if he did he would no longer see his lover.

③ He challenges the sun to admit that he too must be blinded by the loved one's eyes, and asks the sun to report back the next evening to agree that the riches of the world he shines on are in the speaker's bed.

④ The loved one is supreme, declares the speaker. Everything else is a copy. He suggests the sun shine only on the speaker and lover since they are the whole world and their bedroom is the universe.

### WHAT IS SPECIAL ABOUT THIS POEM?

**A** The poem is a metaphysical poem and also an aubade.

**B** It explores a lover's perfection using a complex or **witty argument** or conceit.

**C** The voice is **confident** and **mischievous** and speaks in the present tense.

**D** The poem is written in three stanzas of ten lines each with a **repeating** rhyme scheme.

### AN ALL-ENCOMPASSING LOVE

The poem is a joyful poem and its theme is love, the intense kind of love felt by young or carefree lovers. What do they care for the outside world and the busy sun that dictates time and the seasons? For such lovers time does not exist, and anything of significance or beauty in the world is 'All here in one bed' (20). Their world is complete. Indeed, everything else outside the four walls of the bedroom, even 'Princes', 'honour' and 'wealth' (23, 24), are pale imitations of the loved one.

### THE SPEAKER AND THE SUN

The poem opens with a light-hearted reprimand when the speaker scolds the sun for shining 'through windows' and 'curtains' (3) and waking the lovers. 'Busy old fool' (1) and 'pedantic wretch' (5) typify the way the sun is presented. They are strong images. We as readers can easily associate 'thus', in the second line, with 'fuss', reinforcing the picture of the sun as a fusspot going about his business.

**CHECKPOINT 1**

Name another metaphysical poet from the collection.

**GRADE BOOSTER**

Donne adapts the aubade, a song about lovers parting at dawn, and turns it into a celebration of love. This brings to mind other lovers who part at dawn such as Romeo and Juliet. This is the sort of link between poetry and Shakespeare that you will have to explore in your controlled assessment task.

KEY QUOTE

'Busy old fool, unruly sun, Why dost thou thus, Through windows, and through curtains call on us? Must to thy motions lovers' seasons run?' (1–4)

Contrast this with the speaker. He sees himself and his lover, rather than the sun, at the centre of the universe.

By the third verse the speaker's tone has mellowed a little. He welcomes the old sun in, since its 'duties be / To warm the world' (27–8). And since the world is in the bedroom, then it need only shine there to be 'everywhere' (29).

COMPARE THIS POEM WITH ...

Sonnet 43 – about the quality of true love.
Sonnet 116 – the idea that love doesn't alter.

## EXAMINER'S TIP: WRITING ABOUT TRADITIONAL TECHNIQUES

You need to be aware that metaphysical poetry uses conceits that in turn use playfulness, metaphor, hyperbole and other figures of speech to explore human experience. The sun is used to create the conceit in different ways throughout this poem, since the speaker assumes that he and his lover are more important than the sun, or anything else, and exist outside the usual limitations of time and space. However, you must remember that much of this is tongue in cheek as far as the poet is concerned. The techniques are used to convey the intense, self-centred feelings that lovers have.

Another technique found in the poem would seem to be personification, but it is more accurately apostrophe. As with personification, an idea or object (in this case the sun) is given human qualities. But in apostrophe the speaker addresses the idea directly as though they were in conversation. Read the opening lines of 'The Sun Rising' again, focusing on the questions, to get an impression of the technique.

GLOSSARY

pedantic fussy

# Christopher Marlowe: 'The Passionate Shepherd to His Love'

## SUMMARY

① A young shepherd urges a maid to live with him in a romantic rural setting where they will enjoy nature.

② Her bed and her clothes will be made from the beauties of nature.

③ If these pleasures appeal, come away with him, he begs, to where young shepherds will dance and sing for her.

## WHAT IS SPECIAL ABOUT THIS POEM?

**A** The poem is a pastoral and a **love poem**.

**B** It presents an idealised view of **country life**, using vivid **imagery**.

**C** It has six stanzas of iambic tetrameter.

**D** Each stanza has a regular rhyme scheme.

## THE RURAL SCENE

Since the poem is a pastoral, it does not present a realistic picture of rural (country) life. It is a romantic depiction of 'valleys, groves, hills, and fields' (3), 'Melodious birds' (8) and contented shepherds. All that is needed for a serene happy life is provided by nature. In this respect it recalls the biblical Garden of Eden, before Adam and Eve were cast out. Another important point is the absence of urban life and its corrupting influence. The pastoral is an escape from this.

## ROMANTIC LOVE

The speaker is a romantic, enticing the young woman to 'Come live with me and be my love' (1). But what kind of love does he offer? It is less innocent than it at first seems. Marriage and a future together are not mentioned. Rather he offers 'beds of roses' (9), 'pleasures' (19) and 'delights' (23), all of which suggest that sexual love is uppermost in his mind. You might also like to consider whether the young woman in her 'cap of flowers' (11) and 'leaves of myrtle' (12) is a particular woman or an idealised version.

## EXAMINER'S TIP: WRITING ABOUT RHYTHM AND RHYME

Since the poem is an excellent example of a regular metre and rhyme you should mention how it is composed and the effect of this form. Each stanza follows the same pattern: a quatrain rhyming *aabb ccdd* (and so on, with some rhyming words repeated) in iambic tetrameter. This repetition of rhythm and rhyme gives a musical quality to the poem, which is fitting since 'The shepherd swains shall dance and sing' (21). So we can think of the poem as close to song.

# Christina Rossetti: 'Cousin Kate'

## SUMMARY

1  The speaker describes her life as a naive young woman.

2  A nobleman entices her to be his mistress. She grieves for her loss of innocence.

3  He turns his attention to the speaker's cousin, Kate, and marries her.

4  The speaker becomes an outcast. She compares her life with her cousin's.

5  She sees how, by resisting the nobleman's advances, Kate becomes his wife.

6  The speaker feels mistreated and betrayed. She feels that if their situations had been reversed and Kate had been discarded in the way that she was, she (the speaker) would not have married the nobleman.

7  The speaker's son by the nobleman is her one consolation. Kate, it seems, will have no children, much to the nobleman's sorrow.

### WHAT IS SPECIAL ABOUT THIS POEM?

A  This compelling dramatic monologue is written in the **first person** from the point of view of a country maid.

B  Its powerful themes are **temptation** and **lost virtue**. It is also concerned with the **position of women** in the nineteenth century.

C  Influenced by the gothic, its emotions are **dramatic** and **forceful**.

## THE 'FALLEN WOMAN'

The speaker's feelings towards her cousin Kate would seem to arise from jealousy. However, there are other factors at play. As an abandoned mistress, the speaker is, in nineteenth-century terms, 'a fallen woman'. A woman then had few, if any, rights, and marriage was the main way she survived economically. This gender inequality meant that men could make choices not available to women.

## TEMPTATION

The poem has underlying religious themes related to temptation and sin. Although the speaker has been 'lured' (9) to the nobleman's palace, she experiences 'joy' (10) at being in love. But she is also the nobleman's 'plaything' (12) and leads a 'shameless shameful life' (11). This contradiction can be understood as 'shameless' because she is reckless in her love and 'shameful' because she has broken society's rules.

### EXAMINER'S TIP: WRITING ABOUT CHARACTERS

Note how opposing images are used to depict the two women: Kate sits 'on high' (24), when the speaker sits 'in dust' (29). This illustrates the difference in status between the two cousins. As a Victorian 'fallen woman', the speaker has become 'an outcast thing' (28), an object rather than a human being.

**EXAMINER'S TIP**

Draw attention to the way that the nobleman was not simply the object of the speaker's love, but would also have been her only means of support. As his mistress her position was particularly insecure, and even Kate is 'bound' to her husband through the marriage 'ring' (26).

**GRADE BOOSTER**

Drawing attention to the way the speaker clings to her son in the last verse, and discussing whether or not she is afraid that the nobleman will eventually claim his son, could gain you extra marks in the exam.

## William Shakespeare: 'Sonnet 18'

### SUMMARY

1. The speaker compares his lover to a summer's day, saying his lover is more beautiful and consistent.

2. Summer, he says, can be unreliable in several ways.

3. Unlike a summer's day, the lover will never fade but will live in the poem for as long as it is read.

### WHAT IS SPECIAL ABOUT THIS POEM?

**A** The poem's power lies mainly in its delicate images of a **youthful beauty** that will not fade.

**B** It is a sonnet written in iambic pentameter as three quatrains with a rhyming couplet at the end.

**C** It explores the theme that the lover's **beauty** can **resist time** by living on within the poem.

### IMAGES OF BEAUTY

The sonnet opens with one of the most memorable lines in Shakespeare, a rhetorical question: 'Shall I compare thee to a summer's day?' The loved one is more beautiful and steadfast than a summer's day, says the speaker. A summer's day is inconsistent, too windy, too short, too hot and sometimes overcast. However, many of the images depicting the season, such as 'darling buds' (3), 'the eye of heaven' (5) and 'his gold complexion' (6), are so beautiful that we cannot help but associate them with the lover, and we are told that the lover is more beautiful than these.

### ETERNITY

The sonnet's theme is not about beauty alone: it is about beauty that has an 'eternal summer' (9), and that resists time. This is possible because whenever the poem is read the lover is recreated, and the speaker seems convinced that the poem will live on. It seems he was right, for the poem is still read five hundred years after it was written!

### EXAMINER'S TIP: WRITING ABOUT STRUCTURE

To help you in the exam, remember that in a Shakespearean sonnet the poem presents a particular idea in the first two quatrains. (The lover's beauty is greater than summer.) The third quatrain is marked by 'But' (9), which is a turn or volta. (But unlike the summer, the lover's beauty will never fade.) The rhyming couplet presents the conclusion. (The lover's beauty will not fade because as long as humans exist the poem will be read, 'and this gives life to thee' (14).)

 **DID YOU KNOW?**

This sonnet is part of a group called the Fair Youth sequence (sonnets 1–26 of Shakespeare's larger collection of sonnets). Although the images are often applied to women in the poems, most critics now agree that the loved one is a young man.

**COMPARE THIS POEM WITH ...**

**Sweet 18** – about youth and age.
**Sonnet 116** – the idea that love doesn't alter.

# Elizabeth Barrett Browning: 'Sonnet 43'

## SUMMARY

❶ The speaker describes the different qualities of her love.

❷ These qualities are present in a variety of emotions and situations.

❸ After death, her love will grow even greater.

## WHAT IS SPECIAL ABOUT THIS POEM?

**A** It explores the nature of **true love** with passion and commitment.

**B** The imagery is often startling and has religious connotations.

**C** The poem is a Petrarchan sonnet written in an octave and a sestet.

**D** The voice is **strong** and **reflective**, expressing **religious feeling** as well as love.

**E** The **pace** of the poem reflects the **strength** of the voice.

## THE SONNET FORM

The choice of the sonnet form, in this case the Petrarchan sonnet, is ideal for this poem, since sonnets traditionally focus on love. The first four lines explore the limitless nature of the speaker's love, while the next four look at love from a less dramatic perspective, 'every day's / Most quiet need' (5–6). These two quatrains form the octave. After this comes the volta or turn, leading into the final six lines or sestet, where the speaker recalls her past life and the nature of her love beyond death.

## PACE AND REPETITION

The movement of the poem reflects the speaker's certainty. For example, the opening question ends in the middle of the line (caesura), and is followed by a confident answer and another pause. This gives emphasis to the second line, which then runs exuberantly into the third without a pause at the end of the line (enjambment). The repeating 't' and 'th' sounds in the words (see line 2) help the line to flow smoothly as the nature of the speaker's love is explored.

## EXAMINER'S TIP: RELIGIOUS IMAGERY

You should mention that by using religious imagery the speaker conveys the quality of her love and her belief. For example, her love is measured by 'the depth and breadth and height' (2) of the soul's reach. These mathematical references, which would normally be precise, are the dimensions of an abstract religious idea, the soul, which is beyond understanding. This suggests that the love is beyond measurement, particularly in the context of 'Grace' (4), or God's love and mercy. This connects with the last lines, when the speaker declares that 'if God choose' she will love even 'better after death' (13, 14).

**KEY QUOTE**

'How do I love thee? Let me count the ways.' (1)

**COMPARE THIS POEM WITH ...**

**The Passionate Shepherd to His Love** – an idealised view of romantic love. **Sonnet 18** – the idea that a lover's beauty can defy time.

**CHECKPOINT 2**

What kind of love does a 'childhood's faith' suggest?

**GLOSSARY**

**Grace** in the Christian religion, the love, favour and mercy of God

# Carol Ann Duffy: 'Valentine'

## SUMMARY

① The speaker gives her lover an onion as a valentine gift. She describes its attractive qualities.

② She also describes the onion's disagreeable and overpowering features because she wants to express what she feels about her lover truthfully.

③ She offers the onion as a wedding-ring, then hesitates. She warns that an onion's smell clings.

## WHAT IS SPECIAL ABOUT THIS POEM?

**A** The poem has an extended metaphor, which creates most of its memorable images.

**B** The poem challenges the **convention** of valentine-giving, suggesting that references to the 'rose' and the 'heart' are untruthful clichés.

**C** The poem is written in the **first person** and the speaker could be of either sex, but the tendency is to visualise a woman speaking because the poet is a woman. She is addressing her lover.

**D** It is a **well-structured** free verse poem, with significant **pauses**.

## ONIONS AND VALENTINES

Here the 'red rose' or 'satin heart' (1), the usual symbols of romantic love, are replaced by the onion – initially, a surprising and comic metaphor. But the onion's features are explored in almost every line. It therefore becomes an extended metaphor. While the onion shares some associations with the valentine, such as the 'moon' and 'light' (3, 4), suggesting romance, it more often represents the thornier aspects of love in the poem: 'tears', 'grief' (7, 10) and possessiveness.

## UNPEELING THE LAYERS

The nature of the onion is varied, and the reader can interpret the poem's images in numerous ways. For example, 'tears' (7), the unpleasant side-effect of peeling onions, can also be the tears and 'grief' (10) in a troubled relationship. And 'tears' also blind or distort one's view, as a lover can be blind to the loved one's faults. The onion's strong taste lingers as the 'fierce kiss' (14) of passion does, and though passionate relationships can be 'faithful', there is a hint of menace in the use of 'possessive' (15). It suggests jealousy. Note also how line 17 can have several meanings, depending on the interpretation of 'are'. Does it mean 'for as long as we are' faithful or 'for as long as we' exist?

---

**KEY QUOTE**

'I give you an onion.
Its fierce kiss will stay on your lips, possessive and faithful
as we are,
for as long as we are.' (13–17)

**CHECKPOINT 3**

Name another well-known symbol of love apart from the heart that is mentioned in the poem.

 **GRADE BOOSTER**

If a poem includes an interesting layout, for example with one-word lines or one-line verses, ask yourself what effect this creates and how it links to the poem's meaning.

In the last verse the speaker urges the lover to take the onion, but only if they are willing to. Its inner 'platinum loops' are offered as a 'wedding-ring' (19), along with a warning: marriage can be 'Lethal' (21) – deathly. Like the onion's smell, the ring, which implies permanence, will 'cling' (22) at an emotional level, even if you wish to end the relationship or are betrayed.

## EXAMINER'S TIPS: WRITING ABOUT PACE AND STRUCTURE

You should try to mention the poem's pace and structure. Its rhythm is greatly influenced by the pauses that occur in the poem. Full stops frequently used at the end of lines, and double spaces between lines and verses, encourage the reader to slow down or pause and reflect.

These features also help the voice to sound assured and give it impact. The single-word line 'Here' (6) makes the reader feel that the speaker is offering them, as well as the lover, an onion.

However, remember that enjambment can also change the pace, particularly when similes occur or an image is developed. For example, the thought in the line 'It will make your reflection' (9) is carried into the next line, and becomes the image 'a wobbling photo of grief' (10), suggesting the reflected image in a mirror of someone crying.

**EXAMINER'S TIP**

Remember that a metaphor that continues the image in some way, as in the exploration of the onion, becomes an extended metaphor.

**COMPARE THIS POEM WITH …**

**The Passionate Shepherd to His Love** – an idealised view of romantic love. **Meeting Point** – about the intense feeling of being in love.

# Robert Graves: 'A Frosty Night'

## SUMMARY

❶ It is winter, and Alice has returned home. Her mother is disturbed by her daughter's appearance.

❷ Alice denies that there is anything wrong, but her mother increasingly presses her to explain.

❸ It seems that the mother has been watching, and realises that Alice has been meeting a lover. Her concerns increase, while Alice protests.

## WHAT IS SPECIAL ABOUT THIS POEM?

**A** The poem is an intriguing ballad written as a **dialogue** between **mother** and **daughter**.

**B** The poem's images help create its eerie and mysterious **mood**.

**C** The **language** and style are archaic, suggesting that the poem is set in an unknown past.

**D** The **pace** increases as the poem develops, creating **tension**.

## FROSTY IMAGES

There are numerous wintry images in the poem, from the reference in the title to the 'frosted star-light' and 'snow' (25, 26) in the last verse. These link to the portrait of the ailing Alice as 'a ghost or angel' (23), with its connotations of death. The images increase with the pace in verses four to seven, when the mother is speaking. The moon gapes, the birds are agitated and the branches are green, as though nature has been thrown out of balance. Alice's feverish dancing, despite the thickness of the snow, also implies madness and disorder.

## MYSTERIES

However, the information we have about Alice and the dramatic events comes almost entirely from her mother. Is her voice reliable? She may be grossly exaggerating out of fear for her daughter. From this perspective, the birds' twittering seems unlikely on a frosty night. Alice does tell us that she is about to write a letter. Is she about to do something reckless or will it be a simple love letter? Is the lover real or imagined? Or is the supernatural at work? These ambiguities add to the poem's mystery.

## EXAMINER'S TIP: DOOMED LOVE?

The ballad is often about doomed relationships and there is a marked sense of foreboding in this poem. But which relationship is doomed? Is it the one between Alice and her mother or the lovers? Will the mother/daughter relationship blight Alice's future? There is a suggestion that it might, as the desperate mother clutches her daughter, who exclaims, 'Mother let me go!' (28).

---

'Your eyes were frosted star-light;
Your heart, fire and snow.
Who was it said, "I love you"?'
'Mother let me go!' (25–8)

Although the poem is set in an unknown past, the reader has a strong sense of the characters' presence in the here and now. What technique does the poet use to create this effect?

The ballad is an early poetic form found in most cultures and set to music. The dramatic stories told were often related to actual events, either personal or public.

# John Donne: 'The Flea'

## SUMMARY

① The speaker is trying to seduce a woman, by presenting a far-fetched argument involving a flea.

② He says that since the flea has bitten both of them, their blood has been mixed together.

③ He begs her not to kill the flea. She will be destroying their unity as well as the flea.

④ But the woman kills the flea, and the speaker scolds her for taking its life. She replies that killing the flea is not especially immoral. In that case, says the speaker, allowing him to make love to her is no more immoral.

## WHAT IS SPECIAL ABOUT THIS POEM?

**A** The poem is a clever metaphysical poem.

**B** The speaker uses an amusing **argument** or conceit to seduce a woman.

**C** The **voice** is **confident** and **bold**.

**D** The poem is written in three repeating stanzas of three rhyming couplets and a tercet.

## THE CONCEIT

The flea is an absurd image or conceit, representing the idea of sexual union between the two lovers. When it bites both of them, says the speaker, their 'two bloods mingled be' (4), in much the same way as their bodies would mingle when making love. So the speaker has cleverly turned the flea's repellent nature to his advantage in his attempts to seduce the woman.

## THE HOLY FLEA

As the poem progresses, the flea becomes a 'temple' (13), a holy place for the so-called marriage between the lovers. There are other religious references too. The marriage temple is 'cloistered' (15) within the flea, so it would be 'sacrilege' (18) to kill it. When the innocent flea is killed, the lover's nail is 'Purpled' (20) by its blood, the reference is not only to the woman's fingernail but also implies Christ's crucifixion. In using religious imagery, the poem also pokes fun at the established Church.

## EXAMINER'S TIP: WRITING ABOUT THE VOICE

Part of the poem's success lies in the voice, and you could refer to this in the exam. Its boldness is apparent, from the outset. 'Mark … mark in this' (1), commands the speaker, as he first draws the woman's attention to the flea. 'Confess it, this cannot be said / A sin' (5–6), he says, encouraging her to sleep with him. Whether or not she does, we will never know.

**COMPARE THIS POEM WITH …**

**The Passionate Shepherd to His Love** – an idealised view of romantic love.
**Valentine** – about an unsentimental type of love.

**? DID YOU KNOW?**

Using religious imagery in a poem to poke fun could be dangerous in the seventeenth century – the Church could have accused Donne of blasphemy.

**GLOSSARY**

**cloistered** protected from life's problems; a cloister is a passage running round a courtyard in a monastery or convent

**sacrilege** treating something sacred with disrespect

## John Donne: 'Holy Sonnet 17'

### SUMMARY

1. The poem is about the death of John Donne's wife.

2. She has died young, but since God has taken her it must be for the good. Her death has focused the speaker's mind on heaven.

3. Through his desire for her, he is drawn even more to God. Yet this is not enough, and he wants more of God's love.

4. He wonders why God's love is not enough. After all, God is seeking his soul in exchange for his wife's and is giving him all His holy love.

5. God, he decides, is a little jealous in case the speaker turns to idols or is tempted to love his wife more than he loves God.

### WHAT IS SPECIAL ABOUT THIS POEM?

**A** The themes are profound, and concerned with **love**, **death** and **religion**.

**B** The death of the speaker's wife makes the speaker focus on his **faith**.

**C** The poet uses the Petrarchan sonnet form written in an octave and sestet to set out his thoughts and **explore** them in depth.

### RELIGIOUS BELIEFS

You need to know something about John Donne's religious beliefs at this point in his life in order to understand this sonnet. For John Donne, God's love and life after death were more important than human love and worldly things. However, in this sonnet Donne's focus on his faith does not necessarily mean that he is not grieving for his wife.

### THE ARGUMENT

The poet is trying to find a reason for this death, as most of us search for reasons when someone close to us dies. For Donne, the answer is rooted in his religious faith. He seems to be arguing that God has claimed her, as though God himself is her possessive lover. In other words, God has taken her, despite her youth, because He loves her. For Donne, this is a key point about her death.

### EXAMINER'S TIP: WRITING ABOUT THE VOLTA

You need to understand the volta at the beginning of the sestet. It marks a change in the sonnet's mood. Earlier, the speaker stated that he needed more of God's love. But in the ninth and tenth lines he asks a rhetorical question (without using a question mark): Why should I ask for more of God's love when He gives me all his love anyway? In the sestet he refers to God's 'tender jealousy' (13), as though God is concerned that the speaker might turn to earthly temptations, such as loving his wife more than he loves God.

---

**KEY QUOTE**

'But why should I beg more love, whenas thou Dost woo my soul, for hers offering all thine' (9–10)

---

**CHECKPOINT 5**

Compare the attitude to religion in Donne's 'The Flea' with that in 'Holy Sonnet 17'. Can you guess which one was written when he was young, and which was written when he was older?

---

**DID YOU KNOW?**

The Holy Sonnets (or Divine Meditations) were part of a sequence of nineteen sonnets.

---

**GLOSSARY**

**ravished** seized and kidnapped or raped

# Tony Harrison: 'Long Distance II'

## SUMMARY

❶ Although the speaker's mother has died, his father behaves as if his wife is still alive and this affects the speaker's relationship with his father.

❷ The old man feared the truth, while the speaker knew his mother was dead.

❸ But when his father dies, we find that the speaker has written his name and number in his new phone book and still rings home.

## WHAT IS SPECIAL ABOUT THIS POEM?

A The **themes** of this moving poem are **grief** and the difficulties of coming to terms with **death** and the language is colloquial in style.

B In the last verse, the speaker shifts from describing his father's grief to considering his own thoughts and actions.

C It has a regular pattern of four rhyming quatrains with a slight change in the last verse that accentuates its thoughtful nature.

## THE EVERYDAY

The colloquial language gives a special poignancy to the father's situation in the first three verses. The ordinary features of his life, the 'slippers', 'gas' and 'hot water bottles' (2, 3), made up his days, and he remained isolated from his son and unable to connect with the world after his wife's death. There are no elaborate images, but some phrases such as the father's 'raw love' (8) suggest the depth of his grief.

## GRIEF

The theme of grief is at the heart of the poem. On one level, the old father knew that his wife was no longer present, but he could not accept her absence, hoping that if he kept her possessions and domestic rituals she would somehow return. The son believes 'life ends with death and that is all', yet when his father dies he keeps his number and calls home, even though he knows there will be no answer.

## EXAMINER'S TIP: WRITING ABOUT THE ENDING

Remember to discuss the shift in the last verse when the speaker turns from describing his father's grief to considering his own thoughts about death and the effect of his father's death. This shift helps to emphasise the sharp contradiction between the speaker's lack of belief in the afterlife and his need to contact his dead father. The word 'disconnected' (16) suggests several forms of disconnection: the disconnected phone number, the disconnection between the speaker and his father because they could not talk about his mother's death, and the disconnection between the speaker's belief and his actions. He 'still call[s]' (16) his dead father's number as though he might be able to connect with him once again.

## KEY QUOTE

'I can remember you, our first Fierce confrontation, the tight Red rope of love which we both Fought over.' (6–9)

# Gillian Clarke: 'Catrin'

## SUMMARY

1. The speaker recalls the birth of her daughter and describes the struggle.

2. The two still clash and neither has won.

3. The growing daughter seeks greater independence. Her mother remains protective.

## WHAT IS SPECIAL ABOUT THIS POEM?

**A** The adult speaker is **looking back** on the birth of her daughter.

**B** The theme of the **mother daughter/relationship** is explored in a compelling and honest way.

**C** The imagery evokes the **joy** and **pain** of motherhood.

**D** The poem is written in free verse with some **rhyme**.

## KEY CONNECTION

Gillian Clarke is the National Poet for Wales. The role involves writing work that will promote Wales, and is rather like being the Poet Laureate.

## MOTHER AND DAUGHTER

On first reading the poem, we might think that the mother and daughter's relationship is and always has been a 'Fierce confrontation' (7). But it is an honest portrayal of a mother/daughter relationship, which is also about the 'Red rope of love' (8) – the umbilical cord. It binds the child to the mother, but must be cut at birth. So the two 'struggle' (15) and Catrin defiantly asserts herself. The mother feels the strain of parenthood, but wants to protect her daughter. Skating 'In the dark' (29) is thrilling for Catrin. For her mother it is a metaphor, representing the unknown dangers that lie ahead for her child, something parents the world over recognise.

## IMAGERY

Some of the most unusual images are in the depiction of childbirth. The speaker writes 'All over the walls with [her] / Words' (12–13), a reference to the screams of the birth pains and also to the speaker's creativity as a mother and poet. The 'wild' movements of childbirth are also 'tender' (14) because the mother is overwhelmed with love for the new baby. That tenderness, 'the rope of love' (8), is called up again later in the poem when Catrin challenges her mother. It comes 'From the heart's pool', suggesting both the waters that accompany childbirth and the depth of love felt for the daughter.

## COMPARE THIS POEM WITH ...

**A Frosty Night** – about the relationship between a mother and daughter. **Prayer Before Birth** – about the unborn child.

## EXAMINER'S TIP: WRITING ABOUT FREE VERSE

Like many free verse poems, 'Catrin' does contain rhyme, but the pattern is not regular. It occurs in lines such as, 'All over the walls ... ' (12) and ' ... as you stand there / With your straight, **strong, long** / Brown hair' (21–3). These repetitions help to give the poem a subtle lilt. Alliteration is also present, for example in the use of the letter 't' in the lines 'taking / Turn at the traffic lights' (4–5), and helps the lines to flow easily, particularly when the poem is read aloud.

# Seamus Heaney: 'Follower'

## SUMMARY

❶ The speaker recalls his childhood and his father's talent with the plough.

❷ He remembers how he followed his father, wanting to be as skilled as he was.

❸ Now, his father in old age follows after him.

## WHAT IS SPECIAL ABOUT THIS POEM?

**A** The poem movingly explores the relationship between **father and son**. Another theme is the **connection** with the **soil** through the speaker's desire to plough the **land**.

**B** The poem's striking imagery conjures up **contrasting** portraits of the child and the father.

**C** The poem is written in six quatrains, with a **regular** scheme of rhyme and half-rhyme and a steady **rhythm**.

## FATHER AND SON

On first reading the poem, we might assume that the child is the 'follower' of the title, as he stumbles behind his father, and their positions are reversed when the father becomes an old man and an irritation. However, the relationship seems more complex. The son's childhood desire to follow in his father's footsteps is never fulfilled and he remains 'In his broad shadow' (20). In other words, early memories still haunt the son, so that his father's expectations 'will not go away' (24).

## CREATING EFFECTS

The poem's regular rhythm, 'Dipping and rising' (16), suggests the plough's steady movement as it creates the furrows. The abundant rhyme ('strung'/'tongue' (2, 4)), and half-rhyme ('plough'/'furrow' (1, 3)) help this movement along. Here and there a line stops in the middle (caesura) to emphasise a point, for example when the father is described as 'An expert' (5). Sometimes a line runs on into another (enjambment), which has much the same effect. For example, 'a single pluck // Of reins' (8–9) runs from one verse into another and draws our attention to the father's expertise in guiding and turning the horses, up and down the field.

## EXAMINER'S TIP: WRITING ABOUT IMAGERY

The father's taut muscular body – 'his shoulders globed like a full sail strung' (2) – and his skill with the plough are the focus for some of the most arresting images in the poem. They reveal the speaker's admiration not only for his father but also for those who work on the land. By contrast, the child is clumsy. He is inadequate to the task, as any small child would be. He is always portrayed as a 'nuisance' (21), until the father 'keeps stumbling' (23), as his strength diminishes in old age.

---

**KEY CONNECTION**

The poem is close to the poet's own experience, and several of his poems deal with rural life and the soil. 'Digging' explores themes similar to those in 'Follower'.

**★ GRADE BOOSTER**

Consider the pathos in the image of the old man, his strength gone, as he stumbles after his son.

**CHECKPOINT 6**

Find examples of alliteration in the first verse of the poem.

**KEY CONNECTION**

Charles Causley was interested in ballads, narrative poetry and folklore, and several of his poems involve mysteries. For an example of a poem about the supernatural, read 'Millers End'.

# Charles Causley: 'What Has Happened to Lulu?'

## SUMMARY

1. The child speaker urges the mother to say where Lulu has gone. She seems to have left in the night, taking her money-box.

2. The distressed mother refuses to explain, and she throws a note on the fire.

3. In the night, the speaker heard a quarrel and a car engine roaring.

4. But still the mother will give no genuine answer.

## WHAT IS SPECIAL ABOUT THIS POEM?

**A** The poem is written as a ballad of rhyming quatrains, with a pronounced, musical **rhythm**, which fits the **age** of the **speaker**.

**B** The narrative is told **through the eyes** of the child, who has heard mysterious goings-on during the night.

**C** **Questions** are asked that provide some **clues** to the mystery.

**EXAMINER'S TIP**

When referring to a poem's form (such as the ballad form), always try to discuss what effect it has in the poem, or why the poet might have chosen the form.

## THE BALLAD FORM

The poem is similar to the traditional ballad in its unhappy theme and its simple but driving rhythm. This musical quality is close to the ballad's origins, which were oral. A story was usually told in song, and although images could be memorable, they were often uncomplicated, as is the case here. For example, 'The curtain flapping free' (6) uses simple alliteration and the image is unsophisticated. The repetition of lines and words is also typical and gives intensity to the voice.

## THE URGENT VOICE

**COMPARE THIS POEM WITH ...**

**A Frosty Night** – about the relationship between a mother and daughter.
**Sweet 18** – about youth and age.

The child speaker's repeated questioning of the mother, heightens the drama, though the reader might wonder whether the child's view can be trusted. However, the questioning is so urgent and the child's voice so strong, particularly in the insistent couplet (1–2), that we are inclined to believe the speaker. We can then assemble the clues from each verse – the 'window wide' (5), the 'money-box' (8), the 'note' (11), and so on — to work out the bare bones of Lulu's hurried departure.

## EXAMINER'S TIP: WRITING ABOUT THE MOTHER

You need to discuss the mother's presence in the poem. The picture we have of her comes entirely through the child speaker commenting on her actions, her emotions and her evasion about what has happened: 'I heard somebody cry, mother, … You say it was a gust of rain' (17–20). This leads us to ask what the quarrel was about. What else is the mother hiding? Is she too distressed to explain, or are there other reasons? That there are no answers is part of the poem's appeal.

# Seamus Heaney: 'Mid-Term Break'

## SUMMARY

① The speaker describes himself waiting in the school sick bay for the neighbours to collect him and take him home.

② There he finds his family in distress, and the ambulance arrives with a corpse.

③ The next morning the speaker looks at his younger brother in his coffin and sees the injury caused by a car.

④ We learn that his brother was only four years old.

## WHAT IS SPECIAL ABOUT THIS POEM?

A  The adult speaker is **looking back** on the **death** of his younger brother.

B  The poem's **simple** but **powerful** imagery relates to the themes of death and separation.

C  The poem is written in iambic pentameter as seven tercets, with a single line at the end. The last line, which is set apart, has huge emotional impact.

## THE IMAGERY OF DEATH

From the first, the reader senses that something tragic has happened. The sound of 'bells knelling classes to a close' (2) has connotations of funerals and death. Later images of: 'Snowdrops' and 'candles' (16–17) are linked to the pale face of the dead child, contrasting with the red 'poppy bruise' (19) on his temple and its associations with blood.

## CHARACTERS' RESPONSES

Events unfold in simple but eloquent, and sometimes colloquial, language. The father, who takes 'funerals in his stride' (5), is 'crying' (4); the baby, unaware of the catastrophe, 'cooed' (7) as usual; and the distraught mother expresses her grief in 'angry tearless sighs' (13). The speaker, remembering himself as a boy, looks on, 'embarrassed' (8) by the attention of neighbours, who tell him they are 'sorry for [his] trouble' (10).

## EXAMINER'S TIP: WRITING ABOUT FORM

The poem does not generally rhyme, but it is organised in traditional iambic pentameter with a repeating verse form. Note the effect: a slow, steady regularity that reminds us of a funeral march. Also note the effect of the last line, which lies not only in the revelation that the dead brother was just four years old, but also in its layout. Although it is set apart, it creates (with the line before) a rhyming couplet – one of the hallmarks of a sonnet, which is usually about love. So as well as the theme of death, the love felt for the child is reinforced.

# Jon Stallworthy: 'The Almond Tree'

## SUMMARY

① The speaker is travelling to hospital for the birth of his child. He hopes it will be a son.

② He parks his car under an almond tree and enters the hospital.

③ There, he is told that his son is a Downs syndrome baby. He describes his feelings of shock and disappointment.

④ He describes the gulf between his son and himself and considers the different lives of the patients in the hospital and what might happen to them.

⑤ The almond tree consoles him and he begins to see that his son can enrich his life.

## WHAT IS SPECIAL ABOUT THIS POEM?

**A** The poem achieves its power through a **variety** of **literary techniques** including motif, extended metaphor, simile, repetition and allusion.

**B** Its themes of parental expectation and love are **deeply moving**.

**C** The almond tree is a **central motif** in the poem.

**D** The poem is written in **seven parts**.

## THE STRUCTURE OF THE POEM

The poem begins with the speaker's drive to the hospital. He is full of hope at the prospect of seeing his new baby, whom he later refers to as 'my best poem' (48). He feels a childlike excitement, 'the lucky prince / in an enchanted wood' (5–6). The mood can also be felt in the rhythm as the car speeds along from 'bend to bend' (9). Once inside, the 'bone-white corridor' (31) and the 'shuddering womb' (35) portray a starker reality, when suddenly excitement reasserts itself at the speaker's prospect of seeing his new son.

Then the mood shifts dramatically. With the news that his son is handicapped, the speaker is in a state of shock, so that 'the heart within' (64) him seems to have stopped. The final part of the poem shows him dealing with his sense of loss. As his hopes are shattered, his son seems to drift away out of reach. But he checks his thoughts, and compassion and love assert themselves. He starts to come to terms with the events, recognising that he can be enriched by the experience, not diminished.

## METAPHOR

There are many metaphors in the poem. One of the most important is the image of the speaker in shock in part VI. He is a pilot 'treading air' (69), looking down at his plane, 'the buckled shell' (70) of his hopes. Another important metaphor is that of the hospital as a ship carrying human lives, some 'on board / soon to be lost' (87–8), others 'altered' (90) by their experiences. The metaphors of the plane and the ship connect with the journey taken by the speaker in his car. As forms of transport, they take us from one place to another. The speaker, metaphorically, has travelled from one place to another in his own development. It is a journey from inexperience, 'the caul' of his 'thirty / years' growing' (109–10), through pain, to a greater understanding. He is being taught, or 'fathered' (110), by the birth of his son.

## EXAMINER'S TIP: WRITING ABOUT MOTIF

You should discuss the importance of the almond tree, the title of the poem. It becomes a powerful motif and represents the process of healing and renewal for the speaker. It first appears in part III. The speaker parks his car under its 'shadow blossom' (24), an image of protection with a hint of darkness. It seems to wave him forward, 'with a child's hands' (26), as though aware of future events. It is there again, 'waving' (79) him down to earth, as though guiding him, after he receives the news about his son. Later, in part VII, it becomes an image of birth (and rebirth for the speaker). Only when all its buds (or children) open, including 'a pale / face' (the speaker's son, 101–2), does it fulfil its natural purpose. In the same way, the speaker is 'becoming' (105) himself, being reborn and strengthened through his son.

**EXAMINER'S TIP**

When quoting from the poem, try to embed your quote so that it is part of the sentence and flows easily when you read. There are several examples on these pages.

**COMPARE THIS POEM WITH ...**

**On My First Son** – about the death of a son.
**Sweet 18** – about youth and age.

**GLOSSARY**

**caul** a membrane that sometimes covers a baby's head at birth
**Magdalen Bridge** a bridge near Magdalen College, Oxford. It crosses the River Cherwell

**KEY QUOTE**

'Let them not make me a stone and let them not spill me. Otherwise kill me.' (38–9)

# Louis MacNeice: 'Prayer Before Birth'

## SUMMARY

❶ The poem, which depicts humanity as dangerous and bloodthirsty, is spoken by an unborn child.

❷ The speaker pleads to be protected from the human race and asks to be forgiven for its future sins.

### WHAT IS SPECIAL ABOUT THIS POEM?

**A** Vivid imagery is used to create a frightening picture of the world.

**B** The poem's themes are **inhumanity** and **tyranny**.

**C** Various techniques such as enjambment, caesura, alliteration and assonance add to the poem's **intensity**.

**D** The poem's **shape** has an effect on the reading voice.

**KEY CONNECTION**

The poem is not strictly a shape or concrete poem. It is closer to projective verse. The poems of William Carlos Williams (1883–1963) are good examples of projective verse.

## INHUMANITY

The poem's themes of inhumanity and tyranny need to be seen in the context of the horrors of the Second World War, when the poem was written. The unborn child is the voice of the next generation, begging for protection, support and strength to survive in a brutal world. There is no saving grace in humanity. The speaker even begs forgiveness for becoming human, for the sins it will commit once it is born.

**CHECKPOINT 8**

Can you find any signs of hope in this poem?

## MONSTROUS IMAGES

The imagery depicts humanity as entirely monstrous. The unborn child is at risk from the 'bloodsucking bat' and 'club-footed ghoul' (2, 3) and from drugs, lies, and the medieval instrument of torture, the 'rack' (7). Its future is in danger from bullying officialdom, and from those who would turn it into a 'lethal automaton' (30), a soldier trained to fight. Only the soothing aspects of nature, 'water', 'grass', 'trees', 'sky', 'birds' (9, 10) and a guiding light, can provide comfort and hope.

 **GRADE BOOSTER**

Gain more marks by mentioning the effect of internal rhyme and alliteration in the poem, particularly where they emphasise the grotesque imagery, such as 'wise lies lure me' (6).

## EXAMINER'S TIP: WRITING ABOUT TECHNIQUE

Try to mention that several techniques work together to create a fast-paced anxious rhythm, especially in the later verses. Enjambment is used in several lines, and the poem's shape has an effect on the reading voice and the eye as we quickly follow the ever-shortening lines. In the last verse these techniques also suggest the birth process, with the rapidly repeating 'hither and thither' (34–5). And we are reminded of the waters accompanying child birth, 'water held in the / hands would spill me' (36–7). The final couplet breaks the shape of the poem and slows the urgent pace, declaring that it is better to be killed than born into a grotesque world.

# Ben Jonson: 'On My First Son'

## SUMMARY

❶ The poem describes the death of the poet's seven-year-old son.

❷ The speaker feels that he is being punished by God for investing too much love and hope in the child.

❸ Death is preferable to fatherhood and his son has escaped from life's future troubles.

❹ His son was his best creation, and the speaker will never love too much again.

## WHAT IS SPECIAL ABOUT THIS POEM?

**A** The poem is a moving elegy on the **death** of a child.

**B** The voice is forceful in its **despair** and, by the end of the poem, **resigned**.

**C** It is written in six rhyming couplets in iambic pentameter.

## THE STRUCTURE OF THE ELEGY

The poem has three linked sections. In lines 1 to 4 the speaker says goodbye to his son and explores his death. God, he says has punished him for loving his son too much, and placing 'too much hope' (2) in him. This leads into the next four lines as the speaker's feelings deepen. What is the point of fatherhood? he asks. Death is more desirable. But he seeks comfort in the child's escape from future miseries, and the voice softens in the last four lines. He lays his son, his best creation, to rest 'in soft peace' (9), vowing never again to get too close to anyone he loves.

## TECHNIQUES

The imagery is uncomplicated, but you need to understand the biblical references. The child is the father's 'right hand' (1), also a reference to the 'right hand of God'. There is also a double meaning in the speaker's exclamation 'Oh, could I lose all father now!' (5). We can read it as letting-go of fatherhood, but also as a rejection of God the 'father', or as pleading with God to understand why the speaker questions his faith at such a time. His deep grief is reflected in the epitaph he chooses to mark the grave, 'here doth lie / Ben Jonson his best piece of poetry' (9–10).

## EXAMINER'S TIP: WRITING ABOUT THE EFFECTS OF METRE

Discuss the poem's metre. Iambic pentameter is the most common metre in traditional English poetry and suits the language's natural rhythm and the natural expression of sorrow in this elegy. It is helped along by the rhyming couplets. Even where half-rhyme and pauses are used (for example, 'why' / 'envy'; 'lie' / 'poetry') to give emphasis to the speaker's feelings, the metre continues to flow.

**COMPARE THIS POEM WITH ...**

**Prayer Before Birth** – a poem spoken by an unborn child. **Follower** – about the relationship between a son and his father.

 **DID YOU KNOW?**

The pronoun 'his' was in the past often used to form a possessive. The modern reader would understand 'Ben Jonson his' as 'Ben Jonson's'.

**GRADE BOOSTER**

You could discuss the irony in the poet using poetry to pay a moving tribute to his son, whom the poet regards as his 'best creation'. In other words, he creates a poem to say that creating his son is better (and more important) than creating any of his poems.

# Elizabeth Jennings: 'My Grandmother'

## SUMMARY

❶ The speaker's grandmother kept an antique shop and seemed to value her possessions more than her relationships. As a child, the speaker's refusal to go out with her grandmother left her feeling guilty.

❷ When the grandmother was too frail to keep the shop, she still held on to her possessions.

❸ The speaker feels no grief when her grandmother dies: only the sense of guilt.

## WHAT IS SPECIAL ABOUT THIS POEM?

**A** The themes of family **relationships**, **guilt** and **regret** are subtly explored, and the voice is **reflective**, creating a sense of the past.

**B** The poem is highly **controlled** with a tight structure.

**C** It uses subtle alliteration.

## THE GRANDMOTHER

The grandmother is portrayed as cold, someone who values possessions above relationships. Her identity seems to be entwined with the objects in her antique shop (3–5). When she ages and is unable to look after all her valuables, she seems to lose her sense of self and purpose. Then 'shadows come / That can't be polished' (16–17), and she can no longer see her reflection. Apparently unable to give love, she leaves 'no finger-marks' (23) when she dies. However, she is portrayed through the speaker's eyes and we need to look more closely at the picture painted.

## THE SPEAKER

As a child, the speaker feared her grandmother's coldness, refused to befriend her and felt guilt. Later, when the grandmother dies, the sense of guilt re-emerges. However, 'Only the guilt of what I once refused' (20) can be read with the emphasis on *what* she had refused – which was the hand of friendship. So the child's refusal became a missed opportunity to learn about her grandmother, who seemed to be a lonely woman, surrounded by 'absences' and perhaps 'shadows' (16) from the past. As an adult, this is a source of regret for the speaker.

## EXAMINER'S TIP: WRITING ABOUT STRUCTURE

The poem's structure is tight and regular, as if mimicking the grandmother's tidiness. Each verse is a sestet written in iambic pentameter, making the rhythm seem unhurried and thoughtful. The repeating rhyme scheme ends with a final rhyming couplet in each verse, bringing the verse to a close and also serving to stress the themes. For example, at the end of verse one the grandmother has 'no need of love' (6), and at the end of verse two the child feels guilt at rejecting her.

# Caroline Norton: 'My Heart is Like a Withered Nut!'

## SUMMARY

❶ A woman describes her unhappiness after her experiences of life.

❷ Her heart can no longer feel joy or pain.

❸ In her youth she was optimistic, but misfortune has changed her.

## WHAT IS SPECIAL ABOUT THIS POEM?

**A** The passionate voice reflects the speaker's **sorrow** and sense of loss.

**B** The poem is written in three octaves with a regular rhyme scheme and metre that create **order**.

**C** The themes are **disillusion** with **life** (and probably) **love** and **loss of innocence**.

**D** The first line is a refrain and a simile. It reminds the reader of the **depth** of the speaker's sorrow.

## DISILLUSIONMENT

The theme would seem to be disillusionment with life as a result of 'misfortune' (19). What this misfortune is we are not told. But the mention of the heart in the first line alerts the reader, suggesting that an unhappy love affair or marriage is at the centre of things. Another theme is the loss of youth and, with it, innocence. All the speaker's bright hope has been replaced by 'a dark and mournful hue' (20), from which there seems to be no escape, suggesting that the speaker is powerless to do anything about her situation.

## INNOCENCE AND EXPERIENCE

The simile in the first line compares the heart to a 'withered nut', which then becomes both a refrain in each verse, and a motif for a heart that can no longer feel. All the imagery in the poem evokes pictures of either youthful innocence, 'soft to every touch' (10), or experience, which has made the heart 'stern and closely shut' (11). These contrasts are often made through nature imagery: the 'gentle breeze', 'the sun-lit fruit' or the 'hollow shell' (14, 15, 2).

## EXAMINER'S TIP: WRITING ABOUT CONTRAST

Try to mention the other contrasts in the poem. For example, the speaker's heart no longer feels emotion, whether 'joy or pain' (7), and yet the voice is full of passion and distress. The octaves and regular metre (iambic tetrameter) impose an order on the lines. This contrasts with the expressive language and emotional voice, as if the speaker were trying to order her thoughts and feelings and understand the point she has arrived at in life.

**? DID YOU KNOW?**

During most of the nineteenth century, a woman was under the authority of her father or husband. When Caroline Norton (1808–77) left her husband, he claimed their children and also her earnings from writing. Consequently she became active in gaining rights for married women. The Custody of Infants Act, which gave mothers some rights over their younger children, was passed in 1839.

**GLOSSARY**

**verdant** green and fertile

# Ted Hughes: 'Old Age Gets Up'

## Summary

① The speaker describes the experience of old age as it tries to rise in the morning.

② The body struggles to cope with physical tasks and loss of memory.

③ Eventually old age rises and dresses.

## What is special about this poem?

**A** Old age and different parts of the body are personified, emphasising the **ageing process** and its effect.

**B** The themes of the poem are the **infirmities** that come with age, and **survival**.

**C** The voice is **slow**, in keeping with the theme.

**D** The poem is written in free verse, with frequent **double-spacing** between sections, which helps to **slow** the reading voice.

## Old age personified

Old age, and especially parts of the body, are personified in the poem. Old age 'Stirs … its burnt sticks' (1) or legs. An eye 'Ponders' (3) or contemplates 'Ideas' (4). But these 'collapse' (4) when the eye is startled and the mind distracted by the brightness of the morning light, accentuating the way the body does not function as well as it once did. This frailty and lack of co-ordination are also evident towards the end of the poem, when 'Old age … Pulls its pieces together' is (17–20). But here personification reminds us more of a robot than a human. A robot mimics human action, but lacks its smooth fluid movement.

## Memory

Old age also suffers from 'amnesia' (13) or memory loss: 'the blurred accident / Of having lived' (11–12) implies that the past is vague. The mind searches for the right words for old age to express itself in the present, but words become hard to find and 'evade / Like flies' (15–16). Note here that this might also suggest that the poet is struggling to find the right words to conjure up the image of old age.

## Examiner's tip: Writing about themes

While the main theme is the infirmities of old age, try to mention that the poem also deals with survival. Though death is not far away, particularly during sleep (when many elderly people die), old age still 'gets up', as the title of the poem reminds us. This ability to cope can also be inferred from the line 'Something tries to save itself' (14). It is the survival instinct. Old age 'Pulls its pieces together' (20) and carries on with the ordinary routines of life.

**CHECKPOINT 10**

The light at the window is described as 'so square and so same'. What does this suggest about the kind of life lead by 'Old age'?

**GRADE BOOSTER**

There are many potent images in 'Old Age Gets Up', including a simile and metaphors (such as 'burnt sticks' for legs). Locate these and commit some to memory to refer to as needed in the exam. Remember you will need to say what effect they have in the poem.

**DID YOU KNOW?**

Ted Hughes was Poet Laureate from 1984 until his death in 1998.

# Sheenagh Pugh: 'Sweet 18'

## SUMMARY

❶ A mother observes her teenage son. She considers his youthful perfection and innocence and her love for him.

❷ She imagines herself as an older woman being rejuvenated by his youth.

❸ However, she also sees herself as Mother Time feeding off his youth and warns him against Time's destructive nature.

## WHAT IS SPECIAL ABOUT THIS POEM?

**A** The themes of **youth**, **age** and **time** are imagined through striking imagery and sometimes ambiguity.

**B** The thoughtful and attentive voice has the effect of accentuating the image of the speaker as an **observer**.

**C** The poem is written as free verse with subtle full and half-rhyme in lines of varied length, which suit the voice.

## THE OBSERVER

The mother's presence in the poem is pronounced. She is an observer, watching her son and remembering small details, his 'only scars' (3) where he once 'tried to shave' (4) too early, or his youthful shyness that 'makes [his] words short' (5). These observations provoke a surge of maternal love 'that touches [her] heart' (6), and throughout the poem she considers his beauty and innocence.

## IMAGES OF YOUTH AND AGE

The images of the son describe youth's natural perfection. Its undamaged quality is almost too much to bear, tempting the onlooker to shatter it, as we shatter a pane of glass or unbroken snow. Youth is an undamaged 'canvas' (15), but since beauty is natural, the artist cannot hope to recreate its perfection. Age, by contrast, is sinister, envious of youth. It is presented as 'ivy' (25) that clings to a young tree, sucking out its life. It is also 'Mother Time' (28), another 'parasite' (29) and killer.

## EXAMINER'S TIP: WRITING ABOUT AMBIGUITY

The main themes of the poem – youth, its beauty and innocence – are clear. But there are other threads running through the poem. Time figures in the last section, but its meaning is ambiguous. Do the images of 'Mother Time' (28) suggest the mother as an older woman remembering what youth meant, its 'warm flesh' (23) and sexuality and its alert mind? Are these images a jealous reminder of the past? Or are they admiration for the youthful son? Perhaps both. Time is also destructive. It snatches youth away. Mother Time is a 'predator' (29) and the speaker warns her son to 'stay clear' (30) – to stay young as long as he can.

### KEY CONNECTION

In your controlled assessment you could make connections between the mother and son bond as it is portrayed in the poem and in Shakespeare's *Hamlet* between Hamlet and Gertrude.

### COMPARE THIS POEM WITH ...

**A Frosty Night** and **Catrin** – both are about the relationship between a mother and daughter.

### CHECKPOINT 11

A 'clear, shining pane / of glass' (11–12) is a metaphor for Youth. What metaphor do you think best sums up Age?

# Dylan Thomas: 'Do Not Go Gentle Into That Good Night'

**COMPARE THIS POEM WITH ...**

**Follower** and **Long Distance II** – both are about the relationship between a son and his father.

## SUMMARY

- The speaker pleads with his father to show anger at his coming death.
- He points to the way others – the wise, the good and the wild men – might react.
- He urges his father not to accept death peacefully.

## WHAT IS SPECIAL ABOUT THIS POEM?

A  The poem was **written** for the poet's dying **father**.

B  The poem is a powerful **protest** against **death**. **Grief** as well as death is a theme.

C  It is written as a villanelle, so the **form** is tightly **controlled**.

D  The mood is **sombre**, but the voice is **forceful** giving the poem **impact**.

## THE LIFE FORCE

The speaker's voice is urgent. He does not want to see his father slip silently away to death. He wants him to stand up to the encroaching 'dark' (4), even though he knows death is inevitable. The 'wise' (4), the speaker says, do not accept death meekly even though as individuals 'their words forked no lighting' (5), had no effect in the great scheme of things. The speaker is arguing that even though 'Old age' (2) is powerless in the face of death, it should show a love of life through protest.

## GRIEF

Grief as well as death is expressed in this poem. The speaker is angry at death and unable to accept it as the natural consequence of life. Since he finds it hard to accept his father's passing, he demands a reaction: 'Curse, bless, me now with your fierce tears' (17). This is also the last chance the speaker has to be close to his father. Perhaps he needs a final act of communication with him, to feel his love.

**EXAMINER'S TIP**

Refer to the names of different forms of poetry such as the villanelle, or the sonnet, which is a very common form, but only if you are able to say something about the form and its effect.

**DID YOU KNOW?**

Dylan Thomas's father was a committed atheist, while his mother was a committed Christian. Whether or not Dylan Thomas (1914–53) was a believer is unclear. If he was, it was not one of the usual kind. He did not seem to take any comfort from religion.

## EXAMINER'S TIP: WRITING ABOUT THE VILLANELLE

You should refer to the villanelle form since it is one of the poem's most striking features. It has a highly controlled rhyme and refrain pattern. Aside from this form, the metre (in this case iambic pentameter) is also an example of repetition. Study the poem to see where the repeating lines fall. Then note how the continual repetition builds up to conclude in the final stanza, where it has the effect of driving home the poem's theme, 'rage against' (3) death.

**KEY QUOTE**

'That moment she was mine, mine, fair, Perfectly pure and good: I found
A thing to do ... '
(36–8)

# Robert Browning: 'Porphyria's Lover'

## SUMMARY

① The speaker is looking back at the crime he has committed earlier that night.

② He describes how the woman he loves, Porphyria, visits him and how he strangles her with her hair.

③ He describes the happiness he feels at being able to possess her, as she is, unchanged.

④ He continues to sit with the dead Porphyria into the night.

## WHAT IS SPECIAL ABOUT THIS POEM?

A The poem is a dramatic monologue. Consequently the murderer speaks **directly** to the reader.

B The speaker's **everyday** voice as he retells the events suggests he is **out of touch** with reality.

C The poem is written in iambic tetrameter with a regular **rhyme pattern**, which helps to sustain the **narrative**.

D The speaker's **motives** for the crime are ambiguous and open to various **interpretations**.

**CHECKPOINT 12**

Porphryia's lover comments, 'While I debated what to do' (35). What do you think he is he debating?

## STATE OF MIND

Naturally we look for a reason for the crime. But there is no clear answer. We only have the speaker's perspective, and since he has casually murdered the woman he loves, we assume he is insane and therefore unreliable. But we can look for clues. Porphyria is active, in control. She braves the storm to visit him, banks up the fire and attends to him. He remains passive. He does not rise from his seat. Nor does he speak to her. He is 'one so pale / For love of her' (28–9). Are these indications of illness or only love sickness?

There is also a contrast with Porphyria before and after the murder. She arrives at the cottage in disarray, with 'dripping cloak, and shawl' (11), 'soiled gloves' and 'damp hair' (12, 13). When she is dead, her blue eyes 'Laughed ... without a stain' (45) and her cheek 'Blushed bright' (48). The speaker seems to want to preserve the moment just before she dies, when for him she is 'mine, mine ... Perfectly pure and good' (36–7). Then he can possess her for all time.

**KEY CONNECTION**

In your controlled assessment you could make the link that in Shakespeare's *Richard III* Richard's wife Anne suffers a fate similar to Porphyria, but Anne is murdered by her husband because she is in his way in his pursuit of power.

# IMAGES

Porphyria is beautiful. She has a 'smooth white shoulder' (17), and her movements are elegant. But it is the speaker's preoccupation with her 'yellow hair' (20) that we find troubling. Her hair is mentioned five times in the poem and is of course the murder weapon. The images of her passive beauty as a corpse are also alarming, as is the description of the storm, which opens the poem. The wind is personified. It tears down the elm-tops and disturbs the lake out of sheer malice. (Nature's malice also reflects the speaker's crime.) When Porphyria arrived 'She shut the cold out and the storm' (7). The images contrast the chaotic external world with the apparent peace and security of the cottage. Consequently the murder comes as a shock.

## EXAMINER'S TIP: WRITING ABOUT VOICE

The voice is that of a storyteller as well as a murderer, describing the events before, during and after a crime. It is colloquial and often relaxed, at times disturbingly so, when for example the intimate details of the murder are described. The voice recalls changes of mood the speaker felt, such as his agitation before Porphyria arrived and the surprise he felt when he discovered she loved him, but it remains much the same in tone as it retells the events. In the last line, however, when we are brought into the present, there is a marked shift in the voice. What is the reader to make of this? Does it suggest the speaker feels guilt? Is the tone devilish? Is he waiting for God's approval? Or is he questioning God's existence? The last line could suggest that the speaker is more aware of the seriousness of the crime than we have been led to believe.

## Dylan Thomas: 'I Have Longed to Move Away'

## SUMMARY

1. The speaker is describing how he wishes to be free of conventional religion.

2. He describes how these beliefs haunt him.

3. He fears that if he moves away from the old religion it will still hold power over him, and he does not want to die believing in such a religion.

### WHAT IS SPECIAL ABOUT THIS POEM?

A   Its ideas and images are often vivid and **disturbing**, creating a sense of **unease**.

B   The voice is very **powerful** in its exploration of **feelings**, producing a **strong presence**.

C   The poem is free verse, but with some **rhyme** and a formal **structure**.

## CONVENTIONAL RELIGION

**DID YOU KNOW?**

Dylan Thomas (1914–53) was well known for his reading voice and gave many poetry readings. He broadcast for the BBC and his speaking tours were a great success in America.

One of Dylan Thomas's concerns, which informed several of his poems, was conflicting feelings about Christianity. In this poem the speaker seems to be expressing a dislike, even hatred, of established religion, which he believes has nothing new to say ('the spent lie' (2)) while at the same time not being able to fully reject it. The second verse suggests why this is. Fear that perhaps 'Some life' (12), for which we could read meaning or perhaps power in the old religion, might still have a destructive hold over him.

## GROTESQUE IMAGERY

**EXAMINER'S TIP**

If some lines or images are difficult to understand, think about the feelings they conjure up and what these suggest. For example, 'the old terrors' continual cry' (3) suggests that the poet is exploring fear.

Many of the images in the poem are grotesque. The metaphor 'the hissing of the spent lie' (2) is an intensely physical image. It immediately conjures up a writhing snake. The 'hissing' suggests danger and also a loss of expression and language and therefore meaning. It has other connotations too. The serpent or snake is a religious and biblical symbol (which can be benign as well as evil). Here it suggests the serpent in the Garden of Eden, who tempted Eve. The poet would have been well aware of this significance, deliberately creating such an image to suggest dissatisfaction with a religion that can no longer speak to him.

## EXAMINER'S TIP: WRITING ABOUT STRUCTURE

Refer to the poem's structure. Although the two ten-line verses are written in free verse, they are controlled, with frequent rhyme ('away', 'day' (1, 4)) and half-rhyme ('fear', 'hair' (15, 16)) and a steady rhythm. This gives them clarity and regularity, contrasting with the complex imagery that can be difficult to grasp. The speaker is perhaps trying to order his thoughts so that he can better understand his feelings.

# W. H. Davies: 'Leisure'

## SUMMARY

❶ The speaker asks us what life is worth if we have no time to observe it.

❷ He gives examples of what we might see if we took the time to look closely.

❸ It is a poor life, he says, if we can never experience its beauty.

## WHAT IS SPECIAL ABOUT THIS POEM?

**A** The poem is written in rhyming couplets that create an elegant **form**.

**B** The images create pictures of beauty, often of the **natural world**.

**C** The theme of the poem is the importance of **leisure**.

**D** The voice is inviting and **persuades** us to listen to the poet's words.

## TAKING TIME

The poem seems to stress the value of doing nothing. For our own wellbeing, we should take time 'to stand and stare' (2). What the poem really says is that we should take time to look at the world around us. The title of the poem, 'Leisure', is the opposite of work. Although work is never directly mentioned, we can assume the speaker feels it contributes to a life of worry, particularly if it allows us no time to appreciate the natural world and to relate to other people.

## 'STREAMS FULL OF STARS'

Many of the images in the poem are joyful. They encourage the reader to observe the natural world – from the squirrels' secret hiding places, to running streams that sparkle 'like skies at night' (8). In particular, we should experience Beauty, which is personified in the poem. We can read this to be the beauty of nature and the beauty of human relations.

## EXAMINER'S TIP: WRITING ABOUT CLOSED COUPLETS

You should note that the poem is written in seven closed rhyming couplets. Each couplet holds an idea or image, to create a graceful form that mirrors the beauty expressed in the poem. In the first couplet the speaker neatly sums up the theme in the form of a question. It is answered in the final couplet. The remaining five couplets open with the negative, 'No time'. This echoes wonderfully throughout the poem, reminding us that life is short and that the simple but important things in life can easily pass us by.

### COMPARE THIS POEM WITH ...

**To the Virgins, To Make Much of Time** – youth does not last long, so enjoy the moment.
**To His Coy Mistress** – life is short, so pursue your desires.

### EXAMINER'S TIP

Always reread your work as you write to ensure that you are making sense and are referring to examples from the poem to support what you say.

## Carol Ann Duffy: 'Human Interest'

### SUMMARY

① The speaker has been imprisoned for murder.

② He recalls the circumstances of the crime and how he murdered his lover, who was unfaithful.

③ He describes his grief but denies he is a violent person.

### WHAT IS SPECIAL ABOUT THIS POEM?

**A**  The poem is a dramatic monologue so we have a strong sense of **character**.

**B**  The main theme of **murder** is effectively conveyed through the speaker's idiom and the use of **slang** makes the voice seem **convincing**.

**C**  **Rhyme** helps to move the **rhythm** along.

### TELLING IT AS IT IS?

The language is stark. There are no elaborate images and the murderer's motives for killing his lover are clear: she betrayed him. The use of slang – 'banged up', 'slogged my guts out' (1, 5) – and swearing quickly draw a picture of an inarticulate, violent man, who stabbed his lover. The use of the double negative, 'wasn't … or nothing', serves to emphasise that his 'baby … wasn't a tart' (13–14). It also suggests the speaker's remorse at the consequences of his violent actions, as his lover didn't deserve to die. So while he is fully aware of what he has done, he is unable to grasp his capacity for violence.

### STOPS AND STARTS

Caesura or enjambment occurs in every line of the poem. This creates a jarring effect of short sharp, statements, or a voice that seems to gabble on from one line to another. It is at odds with the formal pattern of rhyme, which helps to drive the rhythm. However, the effect of all these techniques together suits the speaker's violent, troubled character and the way we might expect him to deliver his words.

### EXAMINER'S TIP: WRITING ABOUT STRUCTURE, VOICE AND THEME

You should mention that the poem is a dramatic monologue. Because the character speaks directly to us, we have a strong sense of what he is like and how he views his circumstances. You should also point out that the poet has taken the sonnet form and played with it. The poem is written in fourteen lines, and each line has ten syllables. And despite its gruesome theme of murder, it is also about love, albeit an abusive kind of love.

---

**EXAMINER'S TIP**

Try to discuss how techniques in the poem, such as rhyme and repetition, suit (or sometimes clash with) a poem's meaning and themes, and what effect this produces.

---

**COMPARE THIS POEM WITH …**

**Porphyria's Lover** – about a murder described by the murderer.
**Hawk Roosting** – about a ruthless killer.

---

**CHECKPOINT 13**

What words in the poem tell you that the speaker is out of touch with reality, and why?

---

# Ted Hughes: 'Hawk Roosting'

## SUMMARY

❶ The poem is written from the point of view of a hawk.

❷ The bird considers its position in the high trees and its ability as a hunter.

❸ It describes its power over everything.

## WHAT IS SPECIAL ABOUT THIS POEM?

**A** The poem's effect comes mainly from the depiction of the hawk as a **ruthless killer**.

**B** Personification is used to portray the hawk through dramatic monologue. The voice is **proud** and **boastful**.

**C** The setting emphasises the hawk's **dominance**.

## POWERFUL IMAGES

The images conjure up the hawk as pitiless: 'My manners are tearing off heads' (16). Even in sleep the hawk practises 'perfect kills' (4). Its prey can never argue with it. Its 'hooked feet' (3) and extraordinary sight allow it to fly 'direct / Through the bones of the living' (18–19), or in other words to seize its prey as it pleases.

## ABOVE ALL ELSE

Everything else is beneath the hawk in importance. It sits in isolation above the wood in the 'convenience of the high trees' (5). It does not look down on the earth. Rather, 'the earth's face' is turned 'upward' for the hawk's 'inspection' (8), suggesting that the earth submits to the hawk's power. Even the 'sun is behind' (21) rather than above it.

## EXAMINER'S TIP: WRITING ABOUT THE HAWK

Think carefully about how the hawk is portrayed, and what this implies. In one way the hawk is a perfect bird. Only creatures best adapted to their environment survive, and the hawk is such a creature: 'It took the whole of Creation / To produce my foot' (10–11). Nature has no sense of right or wrong, and nor does it care who lives or dies. At the same time, the bird is personified. This makes the reader see it as having human traits, as a ruthless semi-human killer. In addition, the hawk's powerful voice through the dramatic monologue does more than give it authority. It helps to create the impression that the hawk is in supreme control: 'it is all mine' (14). This can lead us to draw parallels between the hawk's behaviour and human behaviour. Is the poet suggesting that we as humans ruthlessly 'assert' (20) ourselves over all living things?

**KEY QUOTE**

'I kill where I please because it is all mine' (14)

**GRADE BOOSTER**

In Shakespeare's *Richard III*, Richard says, 'I am determined to prove a villain' (Act 1 Scene 1). He is a ruthless killer, like the hawk. Making a link between the play and the poem could be useful in your controlled assessment.

**GLOSSARY**

**sophistry** using clever but false arguments

# Robert Browning: 'My Last Duchess'

## SUMMARY

① The Duke of Ferrara shows his dead wife's portrait to a visitor.

② He is proud of the quality of the portrait, but not of his wife. We learn that he has had her murdered.

③ We also realise that the Duke is addressing an ambassador in order to arrange a new marriage, which will bring a large dowry.

## WHAT IS SPECIAL ABOUT THIS POEM?

**A** The poem is a dramatic monologue. Its power is derived from the **portrait** it creates of the **duke** rather than of the duchess, and this creates irony.

**B** The themes are **power**, **marriage** and **death**.

**C** The poem is written in rhyming couplets and iambic pentameter.

## THE DUKE

The duke's sense of superiority – 'I choose / Never to stoop' (43–4) – derives from his ancient family line. His great power allows him to possess what he likes. For example, he values his wife's portrait more than he values her: 'I call / That piece a wonder, now' (2–3). In this sense she is an object, and her death allows him to control her image. All that we know about her is through him. But ironically, his efforts to depict her shortcomings give us a portrait of him as cruel and demonic.

## THE DUCHESS

The duchess is a young woman 'too soon made glad' (22) – too easily pleased – for the duke's taste. Her lack of regard for his 'nine-hundred-years-old' (33) aristocratic name and her way of treating everyone equally is an insult to him. She is like a child, delighted by small pleasures and admiration, fond of animals or a simple present of cherries. Ironically, had she been more cunning and more aware of her husband's power, she might have behaved differently and survived. It is her very innocence that the tyrannical husband cannot control. So at his 'commands', her 'smiles' are 'stopped' (45–6).

## EXAMINER'S TIP: WRITING ABOUT THE DRAMATIC MONOLOGUE

You will need to discuss the choice of the dramatic monologue. By using this form, the poet is able to present the character of the duke in a convincing and theatrical way. It is as if the duke is centre stage addressing both another character and the reader. As he speaks, the drama unfolds and we learn of his shocking deeds from his own mouth.

# Percy Bysshe Shelley: 'Ozymandias'

## SUMMARY

1. The speaker has met a traveller who has been to an ancient land.

2. The traveller has seen a huge ruined statue, of which only the legs remain standing. Nearby is the broken face, grim and ruthless.

3. The inscription on the base says the statue is that of King Ozymandias.

4. The ruin is surrounded by nothing but desert.

## WHAT IS SPECIAL ABOUT THIS POEM?

A. The poem is a **strong** ironic comment on the themes of **time** and **power**.

B. The speaker's voice **dominates** the poem, but he is **reporting** the traveller's words, who also reports the words of Ozymandias. We do not know who the traveller is.

C. The poem's **effect** partly comes from the voice of the **proud** Ozymandias, through the statue's inscription.

D. The poet has adapted the sonnet form, changing the rhyme scheme.

## TIME AND POWER

The poet delivers a potent moral message through the figure of Ozymandias. Not even the mightiest kings or leaders are gods. They cannot survive time, and those proud enough to think that they can will be disappointed. Not only is Ozymandias's statue destroyed, but also his entire civilization. All that remains are the 'lone and level sands' (14).

## THE SCULPTOR'S ART

By contrast, the sculptor's work has survived. He has understood Ozymandias's nature, his 'frown' and 'his sneer of cold command' (4, 5), and used his skill to create art out of stone. At the same time he has 'mocked' (8) or ridiculed Ozymandias. The artist's skill can still be seen in the ruins, suggesting that art is more powerful and will outlive such mighty rulers.

## EXAMINER'S TIP: WRITING ABOUT IRONY

You need to mention the inscription on the statue's base, since this is where the poem's irony lies. Ozymandias's words 'Look on my works, ye Mighty, and despair!' (11) have rebounded on him and come to mean the opposite of what he intended. He wished to instil fear and awe into other mighty rulers so that they would despair, feeling unable to match his achievements. Instead they despair at the destruction and have to acknowledge that no great power is eternal, since all that is left of Ozymandias are ruins.

### DID YOU KNOW?

Percy Bysshe Shelley (1792–1822) supported the French Revolution (1789–99) and was a radical thinker and pamphleteer as well as a poet.

### CHECKPOINT 15

What does the poem tell you about the poet's attitude to monarchy and also to art?

### GLOSSARY

**Ozymandias** another name for Rameses II, a powerful Egyptian pharaoh

**antique** ancient

**GRADE BOOSTER**

If there is an obvious contrast in a poem, for example between one character and another, there may well be other contrasts, such as a change from a slow rhythm to a quicker one. Being alert to the possibilities of contrasts and discussing them will gain you marks.

**DID YOU KNOW?**

Edwin Muir (1887–1959) was a Scottish poet but travelled and lived all over Europe including in Italy, Czechoslovakia and Vienna. He was a translator and novelist as well as a poet.

**COMPARE THIS POEM WITH ...**

**Refugee Blues** – about Jewish German refugees and their persecution. **Displaced Person Looks at a Cage-bird** – about the outsider in society.

# Edwin Muir: 'The Interrogation'

## SUMMARY

① The speaker is a member of a group of refugees who are trying to cross the border illegally from one country to another.

② They are about to cross when a government patrol appears.

③ While the group are being interrogated, they see people on the other side of the border.

④ The interrogation continues regardless.

## WHAT IS SPECIAL ABOUT THIS POEM?

**A** The poem is written in the **first person plural**, so while we hear one speaking voice we know that he is part of a group.

**B** The theme of the poem is **freedom** (and lack of it).

## THE BORDER

Geographically, the border is a line across a stretch of land. The field in the poem exists without awareness of divisions (18). Politically, the border is a divide between two countries and in the poem the division is also between freedom and restriction. Freedom is depicted in the image of the lovers passing by on the other side of the border (17). Absorbed in each other, they act freely, unaware of the value of their freedom, and also of the refugees' situation. Meanwhile, the refugees, wait on the edge (19) of the border, and as the interrogation continues they are also at the edge of their patience.

## FREE VERSE AND RHYME

Although this is free verse, almost every line is a full end-rhyme (as in lines 1 and 5, and 2 and 6). The exception is the last line, though this could be seen as a half-rhyme, rhyming with the line before. Despite this abundance of rhyme, it is only felt lightly, even when the poem is read aloud. This is because the lines differ greatly in length, creating different rhythms, particularly where enjambment is used. However, the rhyme helps to give the poem a subtle underlying coherence that is also elegant.

## EXAMINER'S TIP: WRITING ABOUT THE FIRST PERSON PLURAL

The use of the first person plural (instead of the usual singular) helps to create the sense of a group of people united, as though the speaker were a part of one body undergoing the ordeal. In this way, it creates a sense of shared experience. By contrast, there is no sense of unity in the patrol. It has a chain of command. The leader is law-abiding and strict, his men rude and un-motivated.

# Vernon Scannell: 'They Did Not Expect This'

## SUMMARY

❶ A young couple suddenly leave from an unnamed place. They have nowhere to stay until they find a furnished room.

❷ Their hopes disappear and they grow apart.

## WHAT IS SPECIAL ABOUT THIS POEM?

**A** **Who** the couple are and **why** they leave remains a **mystery**.

**B** The solemn voice creates a **cheerless** mood and the theme of the poem is **disappointment**.

**C** **Powerful** images, including similes, create a sense of a **harsh** cold life.

**D** The poem is written in four quatrains and a quintain, creating a **regular** structure.

## WHO ARE THEY?

The couple are mysterious. Who are they? Where do they come from? We know that they are in 'youth's season' (2) and that they act on impulse, taking 'the first turning' (3), which turns out to be the 'wrong' one (5). The suggestion is that the young couple are lovers, who have run away together but have little means of support. Consequently their life 'in a cold / Furnished room' (13–14) is hard. Time passes and, disappointed, they turn away from each other and become 'strangers' (20). Perhaps they are a metaphor for relationships in general.

## IMAGES OF HARDSHIP

There is little comfort in the images. The 'endearing word' only burnt 'the tongue' (11), suggesting that the love between the young couple quickly disappears. Lacking romance, they begin 'to believe in ghosts' (14), which are perhaps the memories of what they once had. Their hope (of a happy future) is 'stuffed and put on the mantelpiece' (15), so it has died. Instead, hope becomes fortune-seeking, an escape, either through reading the tea leaves or doing the football pools.

## EXAMINER'S TIP: WRITING ABOUT MOOD

Note that apart from the bright image 'the beauty of youth's season' (2), the mood is subdued and becomes increasingly sombre as the poem progresses. The voice of the speaker is one of experience and of foreboding. Even the title, which is repeated in the first line for emphasis, evokes this sense. While the lovers 'did not expect this' (21), the speaker, it seems, did. The lovers, 'Being neither wise nor brave' (1), have been unable to avoid their situation and the reader is left with the feeling that there was never any hope for them.

**KEY CONNECTION**

The lovers in Shakespeare's *Romeo and Juliet*, like the couple in 'They Did Not Expect This', also act without thinking about the consequences of what they are doing. Considering the different outcomes of each couple's actions is a link you could make between poetry and Shakespeare in your controlled assessment task.

**COMPARE THIS POEM WITH …**

**My Heart is Like a Withered Nut!** – disillusion with life and probably love.
**A Married State** – an argument against marriage.

**CHECKPOINT 16**

Can you find the two similes in the poem? What effect do they have?

# Louis MacNeice: 'Meeting Point'

## SUMMARY

❶ The speaker describes two lovers sitting together in a coffee shop.

❷ They are focused entirely on each other and time seems to stand still for them.

❸ Their surroundings appear to take on new dimensions.

❹ The concerns of the outside world slip away and the lovers have no interest in anything but each other.

❺ The speaker considers how wonderful being in love is and how thankful we should be to experience such emotions.

## WHAT IS SPECIAL ABOUT THIS POEM?

**A** The poem's theme is the **intense** nature of being in love and the effect this seems to have on **time** and **place**.

**B** The unusual images create a **dreamlike** effect.

**C** The poem is written as eight quintains. Its **rhythm** and rhyme scheme create a **steady**, regular movement.

## THE INTENSITY OF LOVE

Although the poem is about love, it is not a conventional love poem about or addressed to a lover or an ideal. There is little information about who the lovers are, and only an exploration of being in love. This exploration describes how the intensity of love seems to stop time, which has disappeared 'somewhere else' (1). The clock forgets the lovers. The escalator, a metaphor for continual movement, has stopped and the bell is silent, its clapper (which beats to time) suspended in mid-air. The lovers have become 'two people with one pulse' (3), creating the effect that they make their own time. They care nothing for the outside world (such as the state of the economy – 'if the markets crash ...' (28)). Place as well as time is distorted. The lovers are 'neither up nor down' (10) but simply in the flow of 'the stream's music' (7) and surrounded by visions of the natural world, although they are in an ordinary coffee shop.

## FANTASTIC IMAGES

The images in the poem are often bizarre and their meanings uncertain. They are highly visual, reminiscent of a surreal film where the camera darts from one dreamlike image to another. The 'camels' in verse four are perhaps decorations or patterns on plates, and the 'miles of sand' might be the table or tablecloth (16). The waltz playing on the radio does not 'sound' but comes out 'like water from a rock' (24) and the 'ash' (26) from the cigarette seems to become the plant it once was.

**KEY CONNECTION**

In Shakespeare's *Romeo and Juliet*, Romeo's love for Juliet is so intense that the world seems distorted. Her 'eye in heaven' is so dazzling that 'birds would sing and think it were not night' (Act 2 Scene 2).

The images are sudden pictures that spring up in the imagination, and are also similar to stream of consciousness poetry and prose. They suggest the way in which the senses and the imagination become sharpened when we are in love and how love makes the world appear a different place.

**COMPARE THIS POEM WITH ...**

**Sonnet 18** – a lover's beauty can defy time.
**Sonnet 116** – the idea that love doesn't alter.

## EXAMINER'S TIP: WRITING ABOUT THE POEM'S STRUCTURE

The poem's rhythm and rhyme are uncomplicated and tightly controlled. This seems very different from the poem's complex images. However, the simple rhyme pattern (*ababa*) creates a hypnotic quality, similar to a chant, and is reminiscent of the magical nature of the images.

The repetition of the first and last lines in each verse and the refrain, 'Time was away ... ', are particularly chant-like. The stress on its first word, 'Time', draws attention to time's importance in the poem – how time is distorted when we are in love.

**GLOSSARY**

**calyx**  a protective layer around the bud formed from the leaf-like parts of a flower

# Philip Larkin: 'Afternoons'

## SUMMARY

1. The speaker describes a suburban landscape. Mothers gather while their children play in the recreation ground and playground.

2. The details of domestic life are described.

3. The mothers' youth is passing and being replaced by parental responsibilities.

## WHAT IS SPECIAL ABOUT THIS POEM?

**A** Important themes of the **loss of freedom**, **responsibility** and the **passing** of **time** are explored.

**B** The slow **pace**, the plain images and the lack of cadence in the voice give the poem a **gloomy** tone.

**C** The poem is free verse written in three octaves, giving it a simple **regular structure**.

## A SUBURBAN LANDSCAPE

The poem is a picture of ordinary lives in a suburban landscape. Mothers are at the playground with their children. In the background are the symbols of domesticity: washing lines, wedding albums and working husbands. Children govern their mothers' lives. They are spirited and active and set 'free' (8) in the playground, while the mothers' youth and beauty are slipping away. The mothers have passed the morning of their lives and reached the 'afternoons' (5). Loss of freedom, the responsibility of parenthood and time are all themes.

## UNFULFILLED LIVES

The mothers are pushed 'To the side' (24) of their lives, as though responsibility is limiting their freedom. The afternoons have 'hollows' (5) or are empty, implying empty lives, while the trees create a border, a line perhaps between the past and the present. Summer, or youth, is passing. 'Behind' (9) the adults are the memories of their weddings, while 'Before them' (15) is a tedious future, as the wind (a chill one, it seems) is spoiling the places where they used to go courting. The new courting couples are young and will arrive in due course.

## EXAMINER'S TIP: WRITING ABOUT MOOD

Note how the voice and the images help to create a mood of resignation, as though the nature of domestic suburban life is inevitably unfulfilling. A good example is in the first line, as the reading voice falls with 'fading'. Again 'afternoons' (5) has a downward movement (and an association with a word such as 'gloom'). Rarely, if at all, do our voices rise as we read the poem, so that the lack of cadence creates a monotonous tone that seems to mirror the monotonous lives.

# Carol Ann Duffy: 'Havisham'

## SUMMARY

❶ Havisham is a furious, resentful woman who was jilted on her wedding day.

❷ She describes her unmarried life, her wedding dress and her distorted reflection.

❸ She no longer has the words to express her anger, but sometimes she dreams longingly of her lover's body until she wakes again.

❹ She feels violent towards all men.

## WHAT IS SPECIAL ABOUT THIS POEM?

**A** The **character** and **speaker**, Havisham, is an allusion to Miss Havisham from the novel *Great Expectations* by Charles Dickens.

**B** **Vivid** and **disturbing** imagery depict the themes of **anger** and **revenge**.

**C** The poem is written in four quatrains as a dramatic monologue.

## ANGER AND REVENGE

The themes of anger and revenge are constantly played out through the voice of Havisham, though these feelings affect no one but herself. She is unable to overcome her sense of humiliation at being jilted many years previously and continually tortures herself. The world has stopped for her.

Desire is also a theme in the poem, though a lesser one. The speaker's feelings are complicated by her need for the absent lover. As well as cursing him in the opening line, she calls him 'Beloved sweetheart', and again in verse three her desire for him continues in her dreams.

## IMAGES OF SELF-DESTRUCTION

Several of the images depict the speaker's crumbling physical appearance, painting a picture of a woman transformed. Her eyes have become 'dark green pebbles' (3), a reminder of jealousy's green-eyed monster and the deadness of stone. The 'ropes on the back of my hands' (4) we can read as the raised veins of age and also the hangman's rope that she would use on the man she was to marry. There are no images of him in the poem, other than as a 'lost' or dead body.

## EXAMINER'S TIP: WRITING ABOUT IDENTITY

Note how the speaker's identity is breaking down. Her image in the mirror is distorted and she spends 'Whole days / … cawing Nooooo' (5–6), unable to accept her situation. In verse three her curses have become 'sounds' (9), as if she is unable to speak, and in the final line she stutters that it is not 'only the heart that b-b-b-breaks'. Her ability to communicate is faltering, and with it a sense of self and self-worth.

**CHECKPOINT 19**

What line suggests that Havisham hates all men?

**KEY CONNECTION**

Ophelia, in Shakespeare's play *Hamlet, Prince of Denmark*, is a picture of innocence, but her situation shares some similarities with Havisham's. She is Hamlet's bride-to-be but is rejected by him and loses her sanity. In the controlled assessment you could draw connections between the play and the poem.

**? DID YOU KNOW?**

In the poem the image of 'the dress / yellowing' (6–7) is an allusion to Miss Havisham's wedding dress that she continues to wear many years after the event in Dickens's *Great Expectations*.

**GLOSSARY**

**spinster** an archaic term for an unmarried woman

# Robert Herrick: 'To The Virgins, To Make Much of Time'

## SUMMARY

① The speaker gives advice to young women to make the most of their youth, because it will soon be over.

② Marry while you are young, says the speaker. It may be too late when you are older.

## WHAT IS SPECIAL ABOUT THIS POEM?

**A** The poem is a lyric poem, and its theme is an imperative to **enjoy** the **moment** because **youth** is short.

**B** The imagery of the **natural world** and youth and age is linked to the poem's theme.

**C** The poem is written in a regular metre of four quatrains, with a simple rhyme scheme *abab* giving it a **steady pace**.

## ENJOY YOUR YOUTH

The poem's theme is made clear in the first line, and can be understood as a message to enjoy the pleasures, the 'rosebuds', when you are young. Youth, 'That age' which is the 'best' (9), soon passes, just as a flower once it has bloomed begins to die. The poem is a well-known example of the Latin saying 'carpe diem', or 'seize the day'.

## ROSEBUDS

The image of maidens gathering rosebuds in the first verse is a simple, carefree and traditional picture of the young. The buds have yet to open fully, like the maidens who have still to experience the full bloom of youth. In verse two the movement of time is like the sun's movement across the skies. The higher the sun rises, the 'nearer he's to setting' (8), just as time moves on.

## EXAMINER'S TIP: WRITING ABOUT PACE

Try to discuss the pace of the poem, its effect and how it reflects the theme. Each verse is written in two metres (with some variations here and there). Generally the first and third line of each verse is iambic tetrameter, and the second and fourth the faster iambic trimeter, with an extra unstressed syllable at the end. The effect is a steady, determined pace kept up throughout the poem (and helped along by the regular end-rhyme). The pace reflects the poem's theme, 'carpe diem', and also reflects the steady onward movement of time.

# Aphra Behn: Song: 'The Willing Mistriss'

## SUMMARY

① The speaker describes how she is taken by a lover to a private shady place among the trees.

② She describes the kisses they share in the warm sunshine and the charms of her lover, and suggests what follows.

## WHAT IS SPECIAL ABOUT THIS POEM?

A  The poem is about **love** and sexual **desire** written from a **female** point of view, but it explores both **male** and **female** emotions.

B  There are distinct pastoral elements to the poem, since the imagery is drawn from an **idealised** view of **nature**.

C  The voice is **intimate** but also **playful**, allowing it to be **assertive**.

D  The poem is set out in two quatrains followed by two octaves, with a simple rhyme scheme and steady metres that suit the **confident** and **playful** voice.

## A LOVE POEM

The setting of the poem is a shady grove where the winds 'Kiss the yeilding Boughs' (8), an idealised rural setting to match an ideal view of love. It would fit neatly the description of a pastoral poem except that here the love described belongs to a female speaker. 'A many Kisses he did give: / And I return'd the same' (13–14) is a clear expression of female sexual desire and pleasure and it is given equal weight with the man's. The poem's main themes are therefore equality and the freedom to express desire.

## THE INTIMATE VOICE

As with the pastoral poem, the voice is intimate. The place where the lovers meet is hidden, 'secur'd from humane Eyes' (5), and yet the reader is invited in to witness the scene. The voice becomes appropriately playful as the lovers 'play / A Thousand Amorous Tricks' (10–11). It just escapes bawdiness in verses three and four, as the most intimate details of lovemaking are only implied.

## EXAMINER'S TIP: WRITING ABOUT GENDER

As well as being a bold expression of female sexual desire, you need to say that the poem is also a desire to be heard as a woman. The speaker is claiming the right to express honest feelings and explore love from a female perspective. This was a controversial act by the poet, since it defied the view that modesty was a prized womanly virtue. In the poem, the speaker describes her lover's charms, much as a man might describe a woman's.

**COMPARE THIS POEM WITH ...**
**The Passionate Shepherd to His Love** – an idealised view of romantic love. **My Heart is Like a Withered Nut!** – about disillusionment with love and life.

**GRADE BOOSTER**

In verse three (6) and four (3) discuss how the speaker refers to herself as an active participant, not a passive one (as most women were portrayed in the seventeenth century).

**GLOSSARY**

**Amyntas** an ancient Greek hero and a character from the play *Aminta* (1573), by Torquato Tasso
**Grove** a shady group of trees
**yeilding** giving in, giving way (an archaic spelling of yielding)

## Andrew Marvell: 'To His Coy Mistress'

### SUMMARY

① The speaker, a young man, is trying to seduce a young woman.

② He teases her, declaring that her hesitation would be understandable if they had all the time in the world.

③ But time and youth are short, he argues, and they should not delay consummating their love.

④ So he urges her to accept him. They may not be able to stop time, but they can enjoy the present while they are still young.

### WHAT IS SPECIAL ABOUT THIS POEM?

**A** The poem is a metaphysical poem structured as an **argument** in three parts.

**B** It uses hyperbole and conceit to **emphasise** the argument and its style is **witty** and **clever**.

**C** It has **powerful** themes about the shortness of life and **seizing the moment**.

**D** The speaker's voice is **strong** and **confident** and the poem is spoken in the **first person**.

**E** The poem is written in rhyming couplets in sets of ten, six and seven.

### PRESENTING THE ARGUMENT

The repeated rhyme and rhythm help to move the argument along in a regular, coherent way: the young woman should accept her lover's advances.

The first stanza opens unhurriedly, as the speaker presents his case. He is responding to the young woman's bashfulness by teasing and humouring her. If time did not matter, he could sweet-talk and court her at their leisure.

In the second stanza the pace increases. The opening word, 'But ... ', sounds a dramatic shift in the argument, and presents an opposing idea: time *does* matter. Its 'wingèd chariot' (22) is never far away, so virginity and bashfulness will soon 'turn to dust' (29) and the lover's passion to 'ashes' (30).

In the final stanza the argument reaches its high point, stressing the course of action to take: 'Now therefore ... ' (33). The young man's urgent message is to give in to rough passion:

'Now let us sport us while we may,
And now, like amorous birds of prey,
Rather at once our time devour
Than languish in his slow-chapt power.' (37–40)

**KEY CONNECTION**

Lines 41 and 42 recall the saying 'Out of the strong came forth sweetness', which refers to the biblical story in the Book of Judges (chapter 14) in which Samson notices that bees have made a honeycomb in the carcass of a lion that he had previously killed.

## LIFE IS SHORT

The main theme of the poem is 'carpe diem' ('seize the day'); take your chances while you can because life is short. Time passing is the enemy of youth, and death is the great destroyer. There is no room for missed opportunity and regret. Defy time, the speaker urges, and take your pleasures when you can.

## WHAT KIND OF LOVE?

The poem is also concerned with the theme of love, but not love that develops over time and that we would call mature. That kind of love is ridiculed, as no more exciting than a slow-growing 'vegetable' (11). The kind of love expressed in the poem is lust, whose 'instant fires' (36) need immediate attention. You could also consider here whether the young woman should be persuaded by the young man's argument or is right to hesitate.

**KEY CONNECTION**

In Shakespeare's *Romeo and Juliet* the lovers' passion is overwhelming. They 'seize the day', but their decisions lead to tragedy. Making a connection between the poem and the play could be useful in your controlled assessment task.

## EXAMINER'S TIP: WRITING ABOUT TECHNIQUES AND THEIR EFFECTS

Make sure you not only identify particular techniques but also show how they create effects and link to the theme. For example, hyperbole is used to create wit. If time was never-ending, says the speaker, he could encourage and flatter for thousands of years and love would become 'Vaster than empires' (12) before it was declared. In this way modesty and hesitation are made to look tedious, reinforcing the theme that life is too short to wait.

The imagery is often vivid and arresting. As the pace increases in the final stanza, passion is depicted as 'strength' and 'sweetness' combined 'into one ball' (41–2), evoking the image of lovemaking and the theme of lust. Perhaps it also suggests the pleasure that comes from having the courage to 'seize the day'.

**GLOSSARY**

**slow-chapt**
  slowly chopped or eaten
**Time's wingèd chariot**  in Greek myth, the chariot driven by Helios, the sun god, that travelled daily across the sky

# Christina Walsh: 'A Woman to Her Lover'

## SUMMARY

❶ The speaker addresses her lover, describing what she wants from a marriage.

❷ She is not prepared to adopt the role of the conventional wife, and outlines aspects of the role that are unequal.

❸ However, if the lover will treat her as an equal, they can have a successful marriage.

## WHAT IS SPECIAL ABOUT THIS POEM?

**A** The poem explores the universal theme of **equality** in marriage.

**B** The commanding voice is helped by the use of the **exclamation** and the imperative.

**C** The images depict different aspects of the **woman's role** in marriage at the **time** the poem was written, all of which serve the husband's needs.

## THE DECLARATION

The poem questions conventional gender roles. It is a demand for fair treatment in marriage. It opens with a rhetorical question for effect (although the question mark is absent after line 5), and the answer is given, 'No servant will I be' (6). So the potential wife offers a clear challenge to the would-be husband.

She argues that compromise – the give and take of a relationship – only comes with equality, and the last verse outlines how true companionship based on 'co-equal love' (26) is the only way forward.

## DRUDGE, ANGEL OR LOVER

In the early verses, most of the images are those of the subjugated woman. She is the domestic drudge, the 'bondslave' (3) or the uncomplaining 'angel' (10) who ministers to her husband's needs, the prettified 'doll' (11) or the wife who will simply serve his sexual needs. The final verse changes the position. 'But', it begins, if the man wants an equal companion, all will be well. The images are in harmony: 'comrade, friend, and mate' (21), they will 'live and work' and 'love and die' (22) together.

## EXAMINER'S TIP: WRITING ABOUT THE VOICE

The commanding voice is important and is helped by the use of the exclamation, the imperative 'Go!' (11) and the repetition of 'If that be ... ' (7, 12) and 'Or if you think' (8, 13). The speaker is not looking for concessions, wondering how small changes can be made to a wife's position. It is the voice of authority. In this sense the roles of the man and woman have been reversed. We do not hear the man's reply, but that does not matter. The voice suggests that if these demands are not met, then the speaker will do without marriage.

# Seamus Heaney: 'Twice Shy'

## SUMMARY

❶ The speaker describes how he and a female companion take a walk by the river.

❷ Though they are seeking a relationship, experience has taught them to be cautious.

❸ However, the occasion is still exciting as they talk together nervously.

## WHAT IS SPECIAL ABOUT THIS POEM?

**A** The poem's theme is **cautiousness** in love.

**B** To depict love, the imagery often draws on the **natural world** for its **beauty** and its **danger**.

**C** The voice is **light** but with a **serious undertone**, conveyed through the **rhythm** and rhyme and the sestets.

## CAUTION

The title of the poem sums up the poem's theme, that those who have been hurt the first time are more careful the second. Both the speaker and his companion are seeking love, to fill 'A vacuum of need' (13), but are afraid of being hurt. So neither says what they really think or feel. Instead they engage in 'nervous childish talk' (28) while holding themselves 'apart' (16).

## THE HAWK AND THE RIVER

Birds occur in several verses, and the hawk and its prey is the most dominant image. It is a metaphor for the dangers of a new relationship, which might be a cause for sorrow, something both the speaker and his companion seem to have experienced when previous loves 'Had puffed and burst in hate' (24). The metaphor of the river is a subtle one, but we feel its presence. On the surface it is untroubled, like the couple who chat light-heartedly, but underneath 'Still waters' are 'running deep' (29) and, like the couple's feelings, are not to be trifled with.

## EXAMINER'S TIP: WRITING ABOUT THE POEM'S STRUCTURE

There are several features you should notice about the structure that help to give the poem a distinctive style. The short rhythmic lines (iambic trimeter) and the regular rhyme pattern (in which each verse rhymes in the second, fourth and sixth lines) give the poem a lilt that mimics the couple's gait as they stroll by the river. This lilt, particularly in the first four lines, also seems to represent the surface optimism felt by the couple. However, in the last two lines of each sestet, the tone shifts slightly and the reading voice steadies and sounds a more serious note, suggesting hidden emotions.

**KEY CONNECTION**

The scarf tied in the style of Brigitte Bardot and the flat suede shoes were fashionable in the 1950s and early 1960s, which suggests that the poem is set at this time.

**CHECKPOINT 20**

The traffic is 'holding its breath' (7) and the sky is 'tense' (8). What do these descriptions suggest?

**GLOSSARY**

**Bardot** Brigitte Bardot, French film actress from the 1950s and 1960s

# William King: 'The Beggar Woman'

## SUMMARY

❶ A squire leaves his hunting companions and attempts to seduce a beggar woman. She is carrying her baby in a cloth wrapped round her body.

❷ She encourages him to carry the baby and outwits him by leaving him to take responsibility for the child.

## WHAT IS SPECIAL ABOUT THIS POEM?

**A** The poem is a narrative poem and similar to a popular ballad or folk song.

**B** It explores the **positions** of both **men** and **women** and **rich** and **poor** in **society,** using double meanings and irony.

**C** It is also a tale about using your **wits**.

**D** It is written in closed couplets, which draws attention to the **rhyme**, helping to create a vigorous **pace**.

## TELLING A TALE

Although the poem is not a tragic tale like many traditional ballads, it has some of the ballad's qualities. It is a narrative of a poor woman and, like the ballad or folksong, it is also musical. The closed couplet, with its *ab* rhyme pattern, lumpy rhythm and many pauses, dominates the poem and adds a note of humour. This suits the mocking tone of the poem perfectly, as the beggar woman outwits the squire, who wrongly thought he could seduce her.

## DOUBLE DEALINGS

The poem has several double meanings. For example, the 'game' (4) applies to the hare being hunted and also to the woman, whom the squire sees as fair game, someone he can take advantage of. The squire is certain that he will be able to seduce the beggar woman but, ironically, it is she who has 'the matter sure' (19), both because she is in control of events, and because she literally makes sure the baby is secured to the squire.

## EXAMINER'S TIP: WRITING ABOUT THE CHARACTERS

You should be aware of the different positions in society held by the squire and the beggar woman. The squire has status, a position that allows him great freedom. Being a man, he also has greater power than a woman of the same class. The beggar woman is powerless. Without money, her standing is below most women's, as well as men's. However, in the poem she manages to gain power by using her wits to trick the squire. This is a common theme of folk tales – ordinary people using their intelligence to survive.

---

**CHECKPOINT 21**

What is the double meaning in the word 'astray' in line 1?

**GRADE BOOSTER**

There is no direct evidence that the squire is the baby's father. However, you could point out that the words ''ere you get another' (45) can be read to mean a second child that he will father, the first being the beggar woman's baby.

**? DID YOU KNOW?**

William King (1663–1712) attended Christ Church, Oxford, where it was claimed that during his seven years' stay he read more than twenty thousand books! (Later the estimate was reduced to seven thousand.) How much he read we do not know, but it is safe to assume that he read a great deal!

# Sir Thomas Wyatt: 'Whoso List to Hunt'

## SUMMARY

❶  A hunter is tired of chasing a female deer (or hind) and lags behind.

❷  He presses forwards, but finally gives up.

❸  In any case this quarry is not his to catch, but belongs to another more powerful man.

## WHAT IS SPECIAL ABOUT THIS POEM?

**A**  The theme is **unattainable love**, which becomes evident as the poem progresses.

**B**  The **hind** is an important and powerful extended metaphor for the **woman**, the focus of love.

**C**  The poem is a translation of a Petrarchan sonnet and well-suited to the poem's theme.

## THE HIND

The hind is a difficult quarry, impossible to capture, and the speaker is so wearied by the chase that he must give up. This is the apparent meaning of the poem. However, as lines 11–14 reveal, the poem is not only about a deer. The hind is an extended metaphor for a woman, and one reason she is difficult to catch is because she is not available to the hunter. Around her neck, written in diamonds, are the words *'Noli me tangere* [do not touch me], for Caesar's I am' (13). For 'Caesar', we can read a monarch or a man of power.

## THE PETRARCHAN SONNET

The poem has an octave and sestet, and follows the Petrachan form. In the octave we follow the speaker's thoughts in his weary pursuit of the hind. Then the mood seems to shift from resignation to conviction in the volta. The opening words of the first line are repeated in line 9, but here the pursuit is a hopeless enterprise for anyone, not only the speaker, since it is the pursuit of an unattainable woman. The final couplet makes this clear, and the hind and the woman seem to come together as a final metaphor for the idea of the untamed.

## EXAMINER'S TIP: WRITING ABOUT THE IMAGES

Trying to catch the wind 'in a net' (8) suggests the fruitlessness of pursuing the woman. But the woman may also fear being caught. Around her neck is a message that reminds the reader that she belongs to (and is owned by) a powerful man. The diamonds are a sign of his wealth, and form a collar by which the woman is led. And yet though she seems 'tame', she is 'wild' (14) like the deer, which is perhaps why the hunter is drawn to her.

---

# William Shakespeare: 'Sonnet 116'

## SUMMARY

❶ The speaker opens by saying that he does not want to present difficulties for those who experience true love.

❷ True love does not change even if the world around does. Nor does it change with the passing of time.

❸ It remains strong against life's problems.

❹ If what the speaker says proves to be untrue, then he has never written and true love does not exist.

## WHAT IS SPECIAL ABOUT THIS POEM?

**A** The poem explores the theme of **true love** by contrasting **faithfulness** with **change**.

**B** The images often present **extreme situations** that include personification and allusion. These accentuate the **profound** nature of the theme.

**C** The poem is a sonnet written in iambic pentameter of three quatrains and a final rhyming couplet.

## LOVE AND CHANGE

Exploring true love is the main theme in the poem and it is contrasted with change. Many of the most vivid images present change. For example, 'tempests' (6) create uncertainty; 'wandering' (7) ships are unreliable. Time is unstable, but Love is not 'Time's fool' (9). Though severely tested, it will never change and will continue 'to the edge of doom' (12). Love will also avoid Time's sharp 'sickle' (10), an allusion to the 'Grim Reaper', a skeleton that carries a scythe and represents death. Both Time and Love are personified but Love is the greater, able to resist Time's destructive power.

## LOVE IS NOT ...

The sonnet frequently describes true love in terms of what it isn't. It does not alter. It is 'never shaken' (6). Its value is unknown. The implication is that true love is tricky to define. The couplet at the end is also clever. It declares that if the speaker is wrong in his description, then the poet has never written and no one has experienced true love. But since the sonnet has been written, what it says must be true.

## EXAMINER'S TIP: WRITING ABOUT THE VOICE

You should note how self-assured the voice seems. It attempts to convince the reader that what it says is right. Declarations such as 'It is' (7) and 'O, no!' (5) are made with force and power. The voice helps to create a serious tone, and despite the frequent caesuras the steady, reliable iambic pentameter continues and enhances the voice.

# William Shakespeare: 'Sonnet 130'

## SUMMARY

1 The speaker describes his lover.

2 Her features and traits are less than perfect, so it would be false to exaggerate her qualities.

3 But there is something special about her that makes her perfect for him.

## WHAT IS SPECIAL ABOUT THIS POEM?

**A** The poem is a sonnet written in iambic pentameter of three quatrains and a rhyming couplet at the end.

**B** The poem is a satire and its effect is startling since it **challenges** the **traditional** sonnet.

**C** The tone is quiet and to the point and suits the low-key voice.

## THE POEM'S STRUCTURE

The poem follows the typical Shakespearean sonnet form. The first two quatrains present comparisons between the lover and several traditional features such as the sun, snow and roses. By the ninth line, however, there is a turn or volta, as the speaker comments on his feelings towards his mistress. Although her voice may not be musical, he says, 'I love to hear her speak' (9), and in the final couplet he fully expresses his love.

## SATIRISING THE SONNET

Sonnets, especially if they are love poems, use elaborate images and hyperbole, often comparing the loved one to some kind of ideal. In 'Sonnet 130', Shakespeare satirises this convention and challenges the idea that his lover is anything other than human. 'Coral is far more red than her lips' red' (2) – or anyone's lips. He goes further. She might even possess undesirable qualities – bad breath, for example. This comes as something of a shock to the reader, but it is a way of drawing attention to an honest portrayal and to the pretence involved in the typical sonnet.

## EXAMINER'S TIP: WRITING ABOUT THE COUPLET

You need to discuss where the real message of the poem can be found. It is in the couplet, where the speaker declares his love. It is his lover's uniqueness that matters. He loves her for herself, for being human. To compare her with a goddess is unnecessary as well as untrue.

Honesty is therefore important in the poem. However, you might also like to consider how the lover might receive such an honest poem. Would she prefer it to flattery?

**KEY CONNECTION**

In Shakespeare's *Romeo and Juliet* (Act 2 Scene 2), Juliet says to Romeo, 'If thou dost love pronounce it faithfully'. You can make links with this quotation and the theme of 'Sonnet 130' in your controlled assessment task.

**COMPARE THIS POEM WITH ...**

**Sonnet 43** – about the quality of true love.
**Sonnet 18** – that a lover's beauty can defy time.

**GLOSSARY**

**If hairs be wires** Elizabethan women often threaded their hair with thin gold wire
**damask'd** the damask rose was brought to England during the medieval period

## Alice Gray Jones: 'Song of the Worker's Wife'

### SUMMARY

① The speaker recalls her life as a mother in a working-class home.

② The work was hard but she devoted her life to her children.

③ Now they have grown up and gone her life seems empty.

### WHAT IS SPECIAL ABOUT THIS POEM?

**A** The poem is similar to a popular song or ballad in its depiction of an **ordinary life**.

**B** The language is colloquial, reinforcing the picture of an everyday life.

**C** The regular metre gives the poem **energy** and **pace** and enhances the voice.

### THE TIDY NEST

The setting of the poem is the 'nest' (8) or home. The mother's ability to keep a 'tidy house' (7) and keep her children clean (which refers to the language they use as well as the clothes they wear), gives her dignity and purpose. It will also give her respectability in the community, and the reference to 'nice and posh' (12) shows an awareness of status. The 'nest' is given great emphasis because the mother expects to be judged by the kind of home she keeps.

### THE MOTHER'S VOICE

As the title suggests, the poem is written from the point of view of a working-class woman, probably of the nineteenth or early twentieth century. The language is colloquial and some expressions, particularly 'mam's' (32), suggest a regional dialect, most probably Welsh since the poet is Welsh. Despite the domestic hardship the voice is surprisingly cheerful, at least in the first three verses. It is also unquestioning. The mother has embraced her domestic life. When its purpose has gone, she, like the workbox, is 'a bird without wings' (31), confined to and by the nest that she has made.

### EXAMINER'S TIP: WRITING ABOUT THE RHYTHM

One of the reasons that the voice sounds cheerful is the rhythm or cadence. Most of the words are one and two syllables, and the rising iambic metre makes the lines bounce along. So even in the final verse, when the children have left, the mood is one of surprise as much as sorrow. However, the energetic rhythm makes the poem memorable.

# Katherine Philips: 'A Married State'

## SUMMARY

1. The speaker says that marriage gives the wife little contentment.

2. Her role is to please the husband and carry out domestic chores.

3. By contrast, remaining unmarried is carefree.

### WHAT IS SPECIAL ABOUT THIS POEM?

**A** The poem is an **argument** against **marriage**, with a **vivid** final image.

**B** It is written in rhyming couplets and a tight iambic pentameter that helps drive along the argument.

**C** The voice speaks with **confidence** and **conviction**.

## MARRIAGE VERSUS THE SINGLE LIFE

In the first four lines the speaker begins the case against marriage. Even the best of husbands are 'hard to please' (2), and though wives hide their true feelings we can read their misfortunes in their faces. The following six lines present the state of the virgin or unmarried woman. Her position is enviable exactly because it has none of the problems associated with marriage. It is 'content' (5) and 'freed' (11) from care. The final four lines emphasise the case in the form of stringent advice from the speaker: renounce love and romance, and stay single.

## MAKING THE CASE

The voice is one of conviction. There is no doubt in the speaker's mind that her argument is the right one. As the advantages of being single are outlined, in lines 7, 8 and 9, we can hear the first word being read as though it were an exclamation: 'No!' 'No!' 'No!' to 'blustering husbands' (7), 'pangs of child birth' (8) and 'children's cries' (9). The advice that follows is then offered freely and with gusto in the closing lines.

### EXAMINER'S TIP: WRITING ABOUT THE LANGUAGE

You need to be aware that the final line is significant. To 'lead apes in hell' was thought to be the penalty for all women who grew old and died unmarried. (At the time the poem was written, the duty of most women was to marry and have children.) But the speaker challenges the idea that it is an unmarried woman who is punished. She implies that a woman's punishment, her 'wordly crosses' (10), exists within marriage, not out of it.

---

**KEY CONNECTION**

You could mention in the controlled assessment that Kate (Katharina) in Shakespeare's *Taming of the Shrew* complains that she must 'lead apes in hell' (Act 2 Scene 1) because Bianca, her sister, is to have a husband instead of her.

**? DID YOU KNOW?**

Katherine Philips (1632–1664) often wrote about love. She considered that there were different kinds: physical love, and the love of friendship, which she regarded as a kind of spiritual love.

**GLOSSARY**

**desemble** lie or trick
**apostate** renounce, deny
**levity** light-heartedness
**leading apes in hell** thought to be the penalty in the afterlife if a woman died unmarried: an ape was regarded as useless for meat, as a working animal or as a pet

# R. S. Thomas: 'Chapel Deacon'

## SUMMARY

① The speaker explores the character of Davies, the chapel deacon.

② He is curious about how Davies manages to appear to be doing one thing while thinking of something very different.

## WHAT IS SPECIAL ABOUT THIS POEM?

**A** The theme is the art of **deception** and Davies is the focus.

**B** There are several rhetorical questions that suit the **investigation** of Davies's nature.

**C** The sonnet form is **adapted** to suit the poet's purpose.

## PRAYING AND SCHEMING

Davies is a complicated and cunning character, able to 'pray' (4) and 'scheme' (5) at the same time. He can focus on worldly things, such as how well his heifer cow might do at the fair, or be attracted by a woman, while praying obediently in church. And he can do these things without apparent concern. He is certainly a hypocrite, but he may also be an object of fascination. There might even be a sneaking admiration for him, suggested in the last line.

## ADAPTING THE SONNET

Though the poem does not follow the pattern of metred verse, it is written in fourteen lines and loosely follows the sonnet form. There are recurring end rhymes, though no traditional rhyme scheme and no final couplet (in which ideas are often pulled together). However, the last line is important since it seems to sum up the exploration going on in the poem. It tells us what it is about Davies that fascinates the speaker: his absolute self-assurance.

## EXAMINER'S TIP: WRITING ABOUT RHETORICAL QUESTIONS

Rhetorical questions are frequently asked, though the speaker is addressing not Davies but himself as he explores Davies's nature. His questions are critical and even rude, and we might think that Davies is being judged. However, the tone of the questions suggests curiosity rather than judgement. The speaker is not asking 'why' Davies is like he is, but rather 'who' has made him that way (which we can assume the speaker thinks is God, given the religious references in the poem).

---

**EXAMINER'S TIP**

Give your own personal interpretation, but for top grades you will need to make close and detailed reference to a carefully selected quotation in the poem to support what you say.

**GLOSSARY**

**chapel deacon** in the Christian church in Wales, someone who helps the minister but is not a member of the clergy

**heifer** a young female cow, particularly one that has not had a calf

# Dylan Thomas: 'The Hunchback in the Park'

## SUMMARY

1. The speaker describes a hunchback who spends his days in the local park, close to nature.

2. Boys playing truant from school taunt him and run wild.

## WHAT IS SPECIAL ABOUT THIS POEM?

**A** The poet explores the life of an **unusual subject**.

**B** The images sometimes appear **unconnected**, so their effect is **surprising**.

**C** There is little **punctuation**, which allows the images to flow.

**D** The poem is written in seven sestets and includes rhyme and half-rhyme.

**E** The themes of **isolation**, **confinement** and **freedom** (particularly of **nature** and the **imagination**) run through the poem.

**F** It seems the speaker may be looking back on his **childhood**.

## THE HUNCHBACK AND THE BOYS

The hunchback and the truant boys are juxtaposed. The hunchback is an outsider who must fend for himself. The 'kennel' (11) where he sleeps suggests confinement. The park, where nature is free, offers him and the truant boys freedom, too, when the gates are unlocked. The boys represent the unthinking, pitiless, but also 'innocent' (40) young. They taunt the hunchback, but seem to act more out of instinct, like animals, than through any plan, as they climb the willows and 'roar on the rockery stones' (29).

## SURPRISING IMAGES

The speaker's thoughts sometimes dart from one idea to another, creating surprising images. The metaphor 'the loud zoo of the willow groves' (22) suggests the noisy truants playing among the trees. Some images are less clear. We might see the hunchback, 'the old dog sleeper' (25), as dozing, while the boys run wild. But who is the woman in verse six? Is she part of the hunchback's dream? Is she a perfect body that springs from his imagination (34)? Or is she a spirit of nature that lives on, 'All night in the unmade park' (37), when everyone has left and the gates are locked?

## EXAMINER'S TIP: WRITING ABOUT PUNCTUATION

You should note that there is little punctuation in the poem. There are only three full stops, so the thoughts not only run on from line to line, but also from verse to verse (enjambment). In this way the images and ideas flow freely, with the effect that dream and reality merge. Where each full stop occurs, the line refers to confinement, as in 'chained him up' (12) or to order, when the park keeper tidies the 'leaves' (24). Confinement and order are the opposites of freedom.

---

# D. J. Enright: 'Displaced Person Looks at a Cage-bird'

## SUMMARY

① The poem describes the feelings of a poet living in an alien country.

② Each day he passes a window where there is a canary in a cage.

③ The bird seems to him to be self-satisfied. He believes that if it were dead he could feel sorry for it. Then he could write better poetry.

## WHAT IS SPECIAL ABOUT THIS POEM?

**A** The poem's themes are what it means to be an **outsider** and also the act of **writing poetry**.

**B** The tone of the poem is one of **complaint**, with a touch of **humour** mainly achieved through the use of **language**.

**C** Several **powerful verbs** and **adjectives** are used to create the imagery.

**CHECKPOINT 22**

What feeling is created by the repeating words in lines 1, 2, 7 and 8?

## THE INSIDER AND OUTSIDER

The circumstances of the speaker and the caged bird are contrasted. To the speaker, being caged seems to be an advantage rather than a handicap. The bird has a home, is 'well-fed' and is literally an insider, unlike the speaker who suffers as one of society's outsiders. The bird belongs. The speaker has no sense of belonging, and yearns for the time he can leave. 'How long?' he asks more than once in the poem.

## THE BIRD

Several striking verbs and adjectives depict the bird. It appears in the window, busily 'tapping' (5), 'flexing' (6) or 'Looming and booming' (4). It is 'Florid, complacent' (10) and 'Feather-bedded' (11) and could be seen as a metaphor for all those people who have the good luck to call a place home. The speaker finds the bird's presence objectionable and, alluding to a line from a poem by Wordsworth, he changes 'more' to 'less' (12) and creates an insult. If the bird were dead, says the speaker, he could identify with it as an 'innocent victim' (16), like himself. But for all his complaint it is the bird that provides the subject for a poem – whether a 'better' (14) poem or not.

**EXAMINER'S TIP**

Always read a poem through first. After you have read it, jot down your impressions and gain an overall sense of what the poem means.

**KEY CONNECTION**

Line 12 is taken from William Wordsworth's poem 'Composed Upon Westminster Bridge' (1802). The original reads: 'Earth has not anything to show more fair'.

## EXAMINER'S TIP: WRITING ABOUT TONE

Note the tone of the poem. Irritation with the bird is clear from the imagery. The use of exclamation marks in the repeating lines 9 and 13 expresses impatience, and the Scots saying 'pawky' (5) helps drive home the outsider's irritation, while also providing a note of humour. This humour is also evident in line 15, when the bird is imagined dead and becomes an object of mock-pity.

# Siegfried Sassoon: 'Base Details'

## SUMMARY

❶ The speaker imagines himself as an army officer during war.

❷ He enjoys a life of luxury behind the frontlines while sending soldiers to their deaths.

❸ He intends to die in his own bed, and cares little for those who die on the battlefield.

### WHAT IS SPECIAL ABOUT THIS POEM?

A The poem is a satire on war and those in command and it parodies popular **marching songs** of the First World War.

B Its bouncing rhythm and regular rhyme are set against the poem's serious war theme.

## GRIM SATIRE

In this poem there is no mention of the horrors of the trenches. Instead, the poem is grimly satirical, allowing the speaker to point the finger of blame. The speaker takes on the persona of a grotesque officer, gorging his 'puffy petulant face' (4) with food and drink while a generation of young men is killed 'stone dead' (9). The pompous 'Roll of Honour' and the officer's apparent concern at another soldier's death (6–7) are a lie. In this way, the poet reveals what he sees are the truths of the First World War.

## POPULAR SONG

The rhythm of the poem is a tight, drumming iambic pentameter. Most of the words are one or two syllables, reinforcing the metre. The rhyme, too, is regular and tight, with a simple rhyme scheme, including a couplet that brings a forceful conclusion. The poem is similar to a popular song of the period called the jingo. Its movement deliberately jars against the serious theme, accentuating the absurdity of war.

## EXAMINER'S TIP: WRITING ABOUT PARODY

More precisely, the poem is a parody of the jingo. It ridicules the style of the patriotic marching song. But its purpose is a serious one since it also mocks the idea of patriotism, not because soldiers should not love their country, but because their deaths are needless. The implication in the poem is that they are being sent to war by incompetent, uncaring senior officers, and the image of 'glum heroes' (3) suggests that the soldiers have become aware of what their fate will be.

**DID YOU KNOW?**

The early poetry of Siegfried Sassoon (1886–1967) was romantic but his experiences of the First World War had a profound effect on his writing, changing his style forever.

**CHECKPOINT 23**

What do you think is the meaning of the poem's title?

**EXAMINER'S TIP**

Try to read a poem out loud to yourself and listen for the poem's 'voice' where it rises and falls, quickens or slows, and what mood it creates.

# Sheenagh Pugh: 'The Capon Clerk'

## SUMMARY

① The speaker complains that her troubadour lover may sing of love, but he is a poor lover.

② His devotion to his poetry and song takes all his passion.

③ Although he writes love poems for her, he is in love with his art rather than with her.

## WHAT IS SPECIAL ABOUT THIS POEM?

**A** The poem is **set in the past** and written in the voice of a medieval lady.

**B** It is a witty pastiche of the medieval ballad.

**C** Archaic vocabulary and **language** patterns are used to make the poem seem **authentic**.

## THE TROUBADOUR

All the troubadour's passion is focused on his love poetry. But it is the kind of poetry that obeys a set of rules, so that the 'sorrows are rehearsed' (23) and the 'virtues numbered' (24). His focus is on 'style' and 'art' (25), which we can understand as artifice or pretence. This would follow the ideas of courtly love. His poems do not express true feeling. By the same token, he cannot express true feeling to his lady and is unlikely to be able to express it to anyone else.

## THE LADY

The speaker, the troubadour's lady, is thoroughly discontented with her lover. She refers to him rudely as a lover who sings about the exploits he never carries out. When it comes to real love, he is passive and self-centred, an impotent 'capon clerk' (1). She speaks in the style of the traditional ballad, so it is her voice that creates the poem, and through her voice the poem becomes satirical, a pastiche of a ballad her troubadour might write.

## EXAMINER'S TIP: WRITING ABOUT THE LANGUAGE

Mention the use of language in the poem. There are several archaic words and expressions. For example, we would say, 'he does not love me' rather than 'he loves not me, sir' (28), or 'he's always complaining', rather than 'to make excuse to suffer' (6). The grammatical structures as well as the vocabulary are meant to suggest the medieval voice, in order to make the poem seem true and convincing.

# U. A. Fanthorpe: 'You Will Be Hearing From Us Shortly'

## SUMMARY

❶ The speaker is conducting a job interview and is asking the candidate a series of personal questions.

❷ We do not hear the candidate's reply, only further comments from the interviewer.

### WHAT IS SPECIAL ABOUT THIS POEM?

**A** The poem is a dramatic monologue that allows the reader to **understand** the nature of the interviewer's character.

**B** It is also a parody of the **interview** situation, derived from the **formal** style and use of **language**.

## STYLE AND FORM

Remember that the poem is not an interview. It exaggerates the style and language of an interview to create a parody, for example in the comment 'Were / You educated?' (25–6). This exposes what the poet sees as the insincerity of the interview situation. The poem is also a form of dramatic poetry. At first we expect it to be a dialogue. But it soon becomes apparent that only the interviewer is speaking, so it is a dramatic monologue. The interviewer seems to be addressing us as well as the candidate.

## THE INTERVIEWER

From the first line, the interviewer is officious. By lines 6 to 9 they have become abrupt and patronising, and from the fourth verse onwards downright rude, as they comment on the candidate's accent, their 'Disturbing' (21) appearance and 'unsuitable address' (36). As the interviewer's insults gather pace, so our sympathies with the candidate and dislike of the interviewer increase. By the time the poem reaches the last line, the ellipsis makes the interviewer's questioning surreal, so that it seems as if, simply by being born, the candidate is unsuitable for the post.

## EXAMINER'S TIP: WRITING ABOUT THE CANDIDATE

The purpose of an interview is to find out about the candidate. So mention that the irony in this poem is that we only hear the interviewer's words, ensuring that we find out about them instead. However, the lengthy gaps after each verse and before the interviewer's additional comments (or asides) give the impression that the candidate does speak. We simply never hear them. In effect, they are silenced (like the reader, if we imagine the poem is addressed to us all, as potential interviewees).

**? DID YOU KNOW?**

The poet Carol Ann Duffy wrote the poem 'Premonitions' as an elegy for U. A. Fanthorpe (1929–2009). Duffy sees the older poet as a forerunner, helping to pave the way and give inspiration to younger female poets.

**CHECKPOINT 25**

Why and how would the poem be suitable to perform as a short dramatic sketch?

**EXAMINER'S TIP**

Don't spend too long explaining what is happening in the poem. Try to draw out the poem's underling themes or ideas and any effects created by features such as imagery.

## W. H. Auden: 'Refugee Blues'

### SUMMARY

❶ The poem depicts the flight of Jewish refugees from Nazi Germany in the 1930s.

❷ The refugees feel their home country is no longer theirs.

❸ They struggle to find asylum in other countries.

❹ The refugees are mistrusted and cannot get past government officialdom.

❺ The public do not seem to care what happens to them.

❻ Everything else around them seems to belong somewhere, but the refugees have no place to go.

❼ In the meantime, Nazi soldiers are hunting for them.

### WHAT IS SPECIAL ABOUT THIS POEM?

**A** The poem's **similarity** in style to the blues gives it particular power. Each verse, of which there are twelve, is a tercet. Blues lyrics are often written in tercets.

**B** The poem is heavily influenced by the **history** of the period. Its themes are **persecution** and **statelessness**.

**C** The poem is spoken in the **present tense**, in which one refugee addresses another. The voice is **forceful** and **compelling**.

**D** The **repetition** of key refrains adds to the lyrical and song-like effect.

### ADAPTING THE BLUES

The blues form is ideal for expressing the wretchedness felt by the Jewish people fleeing from Hitler's Germany in the 1930s. For example, the poem uses everyday language and gives the impression that we are listening to one side of a conversation between two refugees. Talking blues shares a similar quality. We can almost hear the unknown listener agreeing with the speaker at the end of each tercet, rather like call and response, another feature of the blues:

> 'Ten thousand soldiers marched to and fro:
> Looking for you and me, my dear, looking for you and me.' (35–6)

The tercets have repeating words (again, like many examples of the blues). This short form accentuates the highly rhythmic quality of the lines and the easy movement from one stanza to the next.

---

**CHECKPOINT 26**

What does the consul say to the refugees? What does he mean?

---

 **EXAMINER'S TIP**

Remember, where words (or lines) are repeated in a poem, they usually give the poem impact or they emphasise the poem's theme.

---

**KEY CONNECTION**

Try to listen to some examples of blues to fully appreciate the poem. (For example, you can listen to examples of Detroit Blues on the internet – note its slow repetitive rhythm.) This will help you to appreciate the poem.

## THE NARRATIVE PATTERN

In each stanza a situation is set out in lines 1 and 2. So in the first stanza we are told of the wealth and poverty contained in a city. In line 3 the refugees' plight is like a comment on this: 'Yet there's no place for us, my dear, yet there's no place for us'. Each comment is a powerful reminder of the refugees' situation, that their movements are curtailed, their home gone and that no one will help. The incidents and comments build to culminate in the final shocking stanza. 'Ten thousand soldiers', or death squads, are pursuing the refugees. To the modern reader looking back in time, the last verse could be seen as foreshadowing the Holocaust.

**COMPARE THIS POEM WITH ...**

**The Interrogation** – about refugees trying to cross from one border to another.
**You Will Be Hearing From Us Shortly** – about prejudice in the workplace.

## EXAMINER'S TIP: WRITING ABOUT THEMES

You should show how each stanza reinforces the themes of persecution and statelessness. 'The consul' declares that without a 'passport' the refugees are 'officially dead' (10–11). The unknown 'committee' (13) tells them to return next year and the 'public' (16) believe that refugees will take their jobs.

Their desperate situation is also contrasted with that of pet animals who have homes, and with the freedom of 'fish' and 'birds' (26, 28) that have no national boundaries and travel where they will. This is against the backdrop of Hitler in pursuit, like 'thunder rumbling' (19) across Europe.

**GLOSSARY**

**consul** an official living in a foreign country who looks after the interests of those of the same nationality who also live there
**our daily bread** a quote from the Lord's prayer in the Christian religion, used ironically in the poem

# Thomas Hardy: 'In Church'

## SUMMARY

1. A theatrical preacher is ending his sermon and his congregation are emotionally stirred by his display.

2. He departs to the vestry, where he is unaware that a pupil from his Bible class enters and sees him miming his gestures in the mirror.

### WHAT IS SPECIAL ABOUT THIS POEM?

**A** The poem's themes of **vanity** and also **manipulation** are revealed through the preacher's **character**.

**B** The lilting **rhythm** and insistent rhyme create a light effect. They also support the strong **mocking** voice of the speaker.

## THE PREACHER

The preacher is at the centre of his congregation, where he likes to be. His 'voice thrills' (2), and his body 'glides' (5) as though he were walking on air. He enjoys rousing the emotions of his congregation. But his vanity is best revealed when he re-enacts 'Each pulpit gesture' (12) in the vestry mirror. His concerns are more to do with the effect he creates than with the worship he is meant to promote. In a broader sense, the poet is criticising the trappings of religion, particularly where it seeks to manipulate its believers.

## THE PUPIL

The pupil from the Bible class is an innocent, without deceit or the surface 'gloss' (9) of the preacher. He or she represents youthful belief. But they have made the preacher their 'idol' (10), and this creates an ironic twist, since the preacher and congregation seem to be evangelicals (which we can infer from their type of enthusiastic worship). Within this branch of Christianity, idolatry – idol worship – is frowned on.

## EXAMINER'S TIP: WRITING ABOUT THE SPEAKER

Note the speaker's position in the poem. He is not a member of the congregation. He is an observer, watching the proceedings while remaining detached from them. This omniscient or 'god-like' position allows him to see everything that goes on (as though, ironically, it was God that was watching). Also note the speaker's voice. It is scornful, particularly as he watches the preacher engage in his theatrical 'dumb-show' (12). We can understand the absence of words as the emptiness of meaning.

---

**KEY QUOTE**

'And re-enact at the vestry glass Each pulpit gesture in deft dumb-show' (11–12)

**COMPARE THIS POEM WITH ...**

**Chapel Deacon** – about a cunning church deacon. **You Will Be Hearing From Us Shortly** – about the insincerity of a job interview.

**GRADE BOOSTER**

The speaker's presence is ironic, since being omniscient (or 'god-like') he witnesses what the preacher is secretly doing, while most of the congregation remain ignorant of his vanity. Make a note of any other poems in the collection that use this technique.

# Wilfred Owen: 'Dulce et Decorum Est'

## SUMMARY

① The speaker is a First World War soldier describing the appalling conditions of war and recalling a dreadful gas attack.

② He sees a fellow soldier succumbing to poison gas and the image haunts him.

③ If war supporters could see these conditions, he says, they would not tell men that it is glorious to die for their country.

### WHAT IS SPECIAL ABOUT THIS POEM?

**A** The poem's main theme, that there is **nothing glorious** about **war**, is depicted in the shocking images and **chaos** of the battlefield.

**B** The poem addresses all **war supporters** who encourage young men to fight.

**C** The **formal rhythm** and rhyme scheme contrast with the images.

## IMAGES OF WAR

From the first, the images, often similes, are graphic. The helplessness of the men, 'like old beggars' (1) who march 'asleep' (5), is followed by the stricken soldier 'flound'ring' in poison gas 'like a man in fire or lime' (12). This destruction both haunts the speaker and propels him into anger. In the final verse he confronts those who support war, with images of torment experienced not only by the individual soldier but also by a lost generation of 'innocent' (24) young men.

## ORDER AND CONFUSION

The iambic pentameter and rhyme scheme give the poem order. This contrasts with the confusion and terror depicted in the images. We could say that the speaker is trying to control his thoughts in order to depict the chaos around him. Also note the many examples of caesura and enjambment. These threaten to break the ordered movement while emphasising the voice, as if the speaker is struggling to hang on to reality amid the terrible madness of war.

## EXAMINER'S TIP: WRITING ABOUT MOOD

The mood of the poem, while always disturbing, shifts. The sombre tone of verse one, depicting the exhausted soldiers, is created by the downward sound of words such as 'cursed', 'sludge' (2) and 'trudge' (4), as well as the images and pace. Then fear suddenly asserts itself with the short sharp cry of 'Gas! GAS!' (9), giving way to a mood of intense horror and pity, as the speaker witnesses the dying man. Finally, the mood is one of articulate rage at the irony of the patriotic slogan. Owen suggests it is a lie, for there is nothing sweet in dying for one's country.

# Dylan Thomas: 'A Refusal To Mourn the Death, by Fire, of a Child in London'

## SUMMARY

① The poem describes the death of a child during the firebombing of London in the Second World War.

② The speaker seems to say that, in the face of such horror, poetry cannot pay sufficient respect to the child's death.

③ He adds that the first experience of death cuts the deepest.

## WHAT IS SPECIAL ABOUT THIS POEM?

A The surprising title goes against what the reader might **expect**.

B The poem is written in four sestets with repeated patterns that create a tightly controlled **structure**.

C **Death**, **war** and **religion** are portrayed through **bizarre**, dreamlike imagery.

## THE REFUSAL TO MOURN

'I shall not murder' (14) the child's 'majesty' (13), says the speaker. He is suggesting that writing a poem or 'Elegy' (18) cannot begin to do justice to such a horrific death. It is almost to 'blaspheme' (16), to be offensive. But a poem has been written. The contradiction is to some extent resolved when we look more closely. The poem tells us nothing about the event, or the child, who she was or what she was like, which an elegy would do. All we know is that she was someone's daughter. So we could say that these omissions are in keeping with the spirit of the poem.

## OPAQUE SURREAL IMAGES

The language is highly original, creating surreal imagery that is not easy to understand. There are numerous biblical references, particularly to the Old Testament, some of which are linked to nature and prayer. For example, 'mankind making' (1) implies the biblical creation of the natural world. This is in opposition to the destruction of war surrounding the dead child and the speaker. The 'valley' (12) suggests 'the valley of the shadow of death' in Psalm 23, which depicts eternal life. Perhaps we are meant to see continuity between life, death and an afterlife.

## EXAMINER'S TIP: WRITING ABOUT PATTERNS

Note how the poem uses several patterns and techniques. There are three examples in the first verse, where alliteration is adjacent ('mankind making', 'bird beast' and 'last light'), creating soft, gentle sounds. Each verse is a sestet with a similar rhythm and the same rhyme scheme. The rhymes, though different, are all full end-rhymes (such as 'making' (1) and 'breaking' (4)). These patterns give the poem a simple, graceful movement, appropriate to the sombre mood of the poem.

**KEY QUOTE**

'Nor blaspheme down the stations of the breath With any further Elegy of innocence and youth.' (16–18)

**DID YOU KNOW?**

Dylan Thomas (1914–53) was not in the armed forces during the Second World War because of ill health. Instead he worked as a scriptwriter for Strand Films, who produced films for the Ministry of Information.

**KEY CONNECTION**

Dylan Thomas witnessed the bombing of his home town, Swansea, in 1941 and wrote a radio play, *Return Journey Home*, in which Swansea's Kardomah café, a meeting place for writers, musicians and artists, is destroyed.

# Rupert Brooke: 'The Soldier'

## SUMMARY

❶ The speaker, a soldier, imagines that if he dies fighting his foreign grave will become his own country, England.

❷ As he turns to dust, all that is English about him – England's countryside and culture – will be part of the soil.

❸ He will rest in peace, in the knowledge that he has died for England.

## WHAT IS SPECIAL ABOUT THIS POEM?

**A** The poem's theme is the **nobility** of **dying for one's country**.

**B** It is a sonnet written as an octave and a sestet.

**C** The imagery is of an idyllic, personified England, with pastoral scenes.

## SELF-SACRIFICE

The theme is the patriotic idea of self-sacrifice – it is noble to die for one's country. The soldier-speaker is depicted as belonging to the country that 'shaped' (5) him. Whatever foreign place he is buried in will become, metaphorically, English soil since it holds 'a richer dust' (4), his loyal English body. In this way the soldier, united with England, will outlast time.

## IMAGES OF ENGLAND

England is the dominant presence in the poem. It is a rural idyll, a picture without blemish, of countryside and 'English air' (7). Religious images are also evoked. The soldier's body is 'blest by suns of home' and 'Washed' by England's 'rivers' (8), bringing to mind baptism and religious cleansing. And the 'eternal mind' (10) suggests God as well as England, as if the two are intertwined. In the sestet England is finally personified as a loving woman. It is in her care that the soldier rests in peace, 'under an English heaven' (14).

## EXAMINER'S TIP: WRITING ABOUT THE SONNET

Draw attention to the poem's form. Appropriately it is a sonnet, since its focus is love, the love of one's country. It follows the Petrarchan sonnet form as an octave and a sestet. The two are separated into verses, but there is no obvious volta. In the octave the speaker imagines his death and its relationship to England. In the sestet he explores England's virtues and the English soldier at one with his country in death.

## Wilfrid Gibson: 'The Conscript'

### SUMMARY

**DID YOU KNOW?**

Wilfrid Gibson (1878–1962) was one of the Georgian poets (writing in the reign of George V). He wrote the famous poem 'Flannan Isle', based on the real-life story of three lighthouse keepers who mysteriously vanished.

① The speaker watches as doctors give would-be soldiers their medical checks.

② The doctors quickly check each man, unmoved by the fate that awaits them as soldiers.

③ The tired and pale image of one young man in particular affects the speaker.

### WHAT IS SPECIAL ABOUT THIS POEM?

**A** The poem's theme is the **horror of war** and the **lack of concern** of those who send men to war.

**B** The themes are **depicted** through the **disturbing** imagery and are connected to the Crucifixion.

**C** The poem is a sonnet, written as an octave and a sestet and an important volta.

### THE CENTRAL IMAGE

**CHECKPOINT 28**

How is the young man standing and why is he associated with Christ's Crucifixion?

The central image comes in the sestet. The speaker sees the figure of a sickly young man, 'Cadaverous, as one already dead' (11), which becomes a metaphor for Christ's Crucifixion. In the Christian religion, Christ died for love of and to save humanity (so the sonnet, often about love, is a suitable form). The image is also a premonition of the young man's death as a soldier, though his crucifixion, we can infer, will serve no useful purpose.

### THE DOCTORS

**GLOSSARY**

**monocle** a single-lens eye glass or spectacle, no longer fashionable
**cadaverous** very thin and pale, death-like
**conscript** someone who is called to do compulsory military service

The doctors are officers (suggested by the chairman's 'monocle' (7)) and they perform their duties mechanically. They are not interested in the 'endless stream' (3) of men that pass by or 'the living death' (5) they will experience as soldiers. In particular, they do not see the condition of one man. No one but the speaker sees the image, for the doctors are not only indifferent to the sufferings that war brings but also lack the imagination to see the image of Christ in the young man before them.

### EXAMINER'S TIP: WRITING ABOUT THE VOLTA

The poem is a Petrarchan sonnet, but what is most significant about it is the turn, or volta, in line 9. The word 'Then' signals a dramatic shift in the poem as the speaker is confronted by the central image of Christ on the cross.

# Philip Larkin: 'MCMXIV'

## SUMMARY

❶ The speaker sees young men queuing to enlist in the army in 1914 on the eve of the First World War.

❷ It is August Bank Holiday, and everyone and everything seems normal and happy.

❸ People are unaware of the horrors that the First World War will bring.

## WHAT IS SPECIAL ABOUT THIS POEM?

**A** The poem explores the ideas of **innocence** and how **past events** change us. An underlying theme is **grief** for an England that has **gone**.

**B** The speaker is looking back at events with **hindsight**, and the tone is **reflective** and **sorrowful**.

**C** The imagery depicts **everyday lives** before the First World War.

## LOOKING BACK

What drives the poem is the war that has not yet happened. We can think of it as a presence in the poem. Without it, the poignancy of people going about their ordinary lives, unaware of their fate, would be lost. Also conjured up is a sense of an England that is lost. The 'innocence' depicted (25) is a lack of awareness not only of how destructive the war will be, but also of how it will change attitudes, values and culture forever.

## IMAGES OF INNOCENCE AND EXPERIENCE

The image of the men casually queuing to enlist as though it were a 'Bank Holiday lark' (8) belies what we know is their fate, so their position is an ironic one. The bank holiday is portrayed as an easy summer's day. The 'countryside' (17) is, as always, carefree and uncaring about humanity's fate. 'Shadowing Domesday lines' (20) is a complex metaphor. It refers to the Domesday Book of England's distant past, and also to the coming war, with its reference to darkness and the clear association of 'Dome' and 'doom'. 'Lines' refers to the medieval ridge and furrow. It also links to the queues of men in line 1, and both suggest lines of battle and even the lines of soldiers' gravestones and lines of trenches – lengthy holes dug as a defence against gunfire.

## EXAMINER'S TIP: WRITING ABOUT THE TONE

Look beneath the surface at subtle clues for the tone, the 'dark-clothed' (12) children, the 'restless' (21) silence and 'shut shops' (9) foreshadowing funerals and the 'dust' (24) suggesting death. The mood is also reflective and nostalgic for a lost English culture, and what is seen as the ordered levels of society depicted in the stately homes, the servants and the family shops.

# Alfred Lord Tennyson: 'The Charge of the Light Brigade'

## SUMMARY

❶ The poem retells the events of a disastrous battle, the Charge of the Light Brigade (1854), during the Crimean War.

❷ The cavalry of six hundred riders charge into the valley towards the enemy, even though they know a serious error of judgement has been made.

❸ They are surrounded by cannon and shot down, but some still carry on.

❹ The enemy Cossacks and Russians are attacked and some fall, and more of the Light Brigade die.

❺ Those of the Light Brigade that are left return to their positions as heroes.

❻ The cavalry's bravery will be remembered into the future and across the world.

**KEY QUOTE**

'Theirs not to reason why, Theirs but to do and die:' (14–15)

A The poem is a powerful **tribute** to the **bravery** of the men of the Light Brigade. It also suggests that a **dreadful mistake** was made by foolhardy senior officers.

B The poem achieves its **vivid effect** by blending a wide range of **techniques** to evoke the picture of a battle, including repetition, alliteration and assonance. An important allusion is also made.

C The **rhythm** and **pace** is very bold, and is helped along by the frequent use of rhyme to create a pounding movement.

**CHECKPOINT 29**

Which line suggests that the ordinary soldier was not to blame for the events?

## RIDING INTO BATTLE

Many techniques are used in the poem to create the picture of the battle charge. The swift, intense metre, with the stress at the beginning of each foot, helps to create the picture of the cavalry and the pounding horses' hooves. The rhyme, particularly the repeating full rhyme, over three lines, such as 'reply', 'why', 'die' (13, 14, 15), could sound excessive. Instead, it enhances the dramatic effect of men plunging towards their death, apparently without hesitation. So it also helps the poet to depict bravery, a major concern of Tennyson's when writing the poem.

## HISTORICAL CONTEXT

**? DID YOU KNOW?**

On publication in 1854, Tennyson's poem became immediately popular and kept the Charge of the Light Brigade in the public eye. A film of the events was made in 1936 starring Errol Flynn, and again in 1968 starring Trevor Howard.

The use of terms such as 'league', reference to 'sabres' and the fact that the soldiers 'Rode' on horseback into the guns all emphasise the historical context of the event to the modern reader.

## REPETITION, REPETITION

Apart from the repeating rhythm, the poem is full of the repetition of words and lines. Again, this helps to drive home the image of the charge and the sense of imminent death. However, it also conveys the soldiers' mind-set, to act together under orders, without question, however foolish those orders might be. The refrain 'Rode the six hundred', which concludes each verse, with some variation, has the effect of emphasising the soldiers as a unit or one body and reminding us of who this unit was. (Indeed, the expressions 'the six hundred' and 'the Light Brigade' came to mean one and the same thing among the Victorian public.) However, highlighting the cavalry's bravery and endurance under adversity also has the effect of glorifying war, and admiring it. The modern reader has difficulty identifying with this position. We are more likely to think of the individual soldier's trauma and breakdown. But to the Victorians, this collective sense of the glory of war would have been the norm, something the poet would have been well aware of.

## EXAMINER'S TIP: SOUND EFFECTS

Draw attention to the sound effects that come from the use of alliteration in particular. Examples tend to be used heavily in certain parts of the poem. The sibilant is frequently used, for example in verse three, 'Stormed at with shot and shell' (22), and again in verse five, so that we can almost hear the hissing of the bullets as they skim through the air. But the effect of the sibilant changes in verse four: 'Reeled from the sabre-stroke / Shatter'd and sundered'. As the pace slows, the alliteration supports the image of the sword slicing and then bringing down the enemy. Note also how the reading voice literally drops when saying 'un' in 'sundered'. For the modern reader, it is a poignant image because we imagine an individual soldier's death.

**GRADE BOOSTER**

Note the contrast between the men as they sing on their way to the front and the image of them creeping back at the end of the poem, shattered by war. There is no one to greet them, as if their pain is an embarrassment and not to be spoken of, like 'wrongs hushed-up' (11).

# Wilfred Owen: 'The Send-Off'

## SUMMARY

① The speaker describes troops making their way to the railway station to leave for the battlefield.

② They have just come from a sending-off ceremony, where they were given white flowers.

③ Now they are alone, watched only by railway porters and a tramp.

④ The speaker considers their fate, knowing that only a few will return.

## WHAT IS SPECIAL ABOUT THIS POEM?

**A** The poem is written in **hindsight** and its theme is the **pity** and **grief** of war.

**B** The mood is **solemn** and **troubling**, conveyed through the moving images and the simple **structure** of the poem, written in tercets and couplets.

**KEY CONNECTION**

*Men Who March Away: Poems of the First World War* (edited by I. M. Parsons, 1965) contains poems by all the major First World War poets, including Wilfred Owen. It is still available.

## TOO FEW

The public and soldiers are unprepared for how their lives will be forever altered. The speaker, aware of what is to come, seems to carry the weight of this knowledge, and there is a deep sense of grief in the voice throughout the poem. It is felt particularly in the question and answer in the last tercet. The repetition and emphasis of 'few', the few who will return, reveals just how destructive this war will be.

## THE SHADOW OF WAR

From the first line, the image of 'close darkening lanes' (1) suggests the shadow of war. The men sing to keep up their spirits – the adjective 'grimly' (3) implies that they have some inkling of their fate – and they wear white 'wreath and spray' (4), given by women and meant as symbols of good luck (and note that 'white' contrasts with the 'darkening lanes'). But white wreaths are traditionally symbols of bereavement, and in lines 14 and 15 the speaker imagines the sense of cruel irony the soldiers might feel, at the reality of war and the flowers' true meaning. The image, 'Their breasts were stuck' (4), then takes on a disturbing significance, for soldiers often died from bayonet wounds.

**GLOSSARY**

**siding-shed** the shed where trains are kept at the side of the railway track

**porter** a person employed to carry travellers' bags

**front** the frontline of a battlefield, where the army is nearest to the enemy

## EXAMINER'S TIP: WRITING ABOUT THE MOVEMENT OF THE POEM

The regular pattern of tercets and couplets, the full end-rhyme and little cadence, gives the poem a measured pace. It is like a slow march or requiem. We can almost hear a single repeating drum beat in the background that strikes a note of grief. The pace fits perfectly with the mood and theme of the poem.

# Thomas Hardy: 'The Man He Killed'

## SUMMARY

❶ The speaker, a soldier, describes how he has shot an enemy soldier.

❷ Had they met in another place and time, they would probably have shared a drink together.

❸ The soldier imagines that their reasons for enlisting were probably similar, that they both needed work and casually decided to join up.

❹ He considers again how odd war is. You shoot a man who could in another context have been your friend.

## WHAT IS SPECIAL ABOUT THIS POEM?

**A** The theme of the poem is the **absurdity of war** and how sometimes our **circumstances** govern what we do.

**B** The language is the vernacular of an **ordinary man** and this, along with the simple rhythm and rhyme scheme, makes the poem ironic when contrasted with the theme.

## FRIEND OR FOE?

The speaker finds himself in a situation he is unprepared for. In battle he is expected to kill the enemy, but when he faces him, he begins to see that the enemy is a man like himself, not his 'foe' (10). So why did he enlist? Because he was poor and unemployed, and these may well have been his enemy's reasons too. When the speaker tries to justify his actions, in verse three, he falters and doubts that he can. The poet is saying that the ordinary soldier is powerless (whatever side he is on). He must carry out orders to kill, whatever the reasons.

## A CHOICE OF STYLE

The rhythm, helped by the everyday language and simple rhyme pattern (*abab*), bounces happily along, rather like a playground chant or nursery rhyme. It reflects the speaker's simple nature. At the same time, it contrasts dramatically with the theme of war and the death of the enemy soldier, emphasising the ironic nature of the speaker's situation – that he is expected to kill someone much like himself.

## EXAMINER'S TIP: WRITING ABOUT IRONY

Make sure you mention the most obvious example of irony in the poem. It is the description of war as 'quaint and curious' (17), an odd description. War is deadly, and the poet is well aware of this. But placed in the speaker's mouth, this phrase reveals his lack of awareness about the reality of war.

---

**KEY CONNECTION**

In the controlled assessment you could make connections between Romeo's murder of Tybalt, Juliet's cousin, in *Romeo and Juliet*, and the soldier's attitude to killing his enemy, a man like himself.

---

**? DID YOU KNOW?**

Thomas Hardy (1840–1928) wrote the poem with the Boer War (1899–1902) in mind, which he was against. However, the experience described in the poem could apply to any war.

---

**GLOSSARY**

**nipperkin** a glass of spirits such as whisky

**'list** enlist; to join the armed forces

**traps** probably a reference to animals traps (the speaker may have been a poacher, or a gamekeeper)

# Thomas Hardy: 'Drummer Hodge'

## SUMMARY

① The speaker describes the burial of a young drummer boy in South Africa.

② Drummer Hodge had recently come from Britain and knew nothing about South Africa, where he died.

③ However, he will be a part of the landscape forever and the stars above him will be his.

## WHAT IS SPECIAL ABOUT THIS POEM?

**A** The theme of the poem is that life seems to matter little during war.

**B** The voice is **sad** and **thoughtful**, so that Drummer Hodge's death is told with respect.

**C** The images create powerful connections between earth and heaven.

**D** The regular **rhythm** is broken by enjambment, caesura and dashes, helping to slow the **pace**.

## WAR DEAD

**DID YOU KNOW?**

During the Boer War (1899–1902) children were still able to enlist, usually as musicians. Drummers, buglers and trumpet players were around thirteen or fourteen years old but could be as young as twelve.

No one is concerned enough to bury the young drummer with care. He is laid to rest 'just as found' (2). He has no coffin, and nothing to mark his grave except the crest of a small hill – which suggests his burial mound. His treatment implies that life during war is cheap. Drummer Hodge knows nothing of Africa, yet ironically the land in which he dies will become his permanent home and his body will provide nourishment for an unknown tree in a strange landscape. We are left with the impression of a wasted life.

## LAND AND STARS

**DID YOU KNOW?**

Afrikaans is a language spoken in South Africa that is descended from Dutch.

The Afrikaans vocabulary is to do with land. It not only creates the impression of unfamiliar territory, on which battles have been fought, but also emphasises that battles can be fought over the ownership of unfamiliar land. Stars are the stimulus for important imagery too, suggesting a relationship between the earth and heaven. Drummer Hodge is far from home, and above him are unknown stars – except that in the last line they become 'his stars eternally' (18), watchful spirits shining over him, perhaps.

**GLOSSARY**

**kopje-crest** a small isolated hill
**veldt** open grassland
**karoo** plateau in South Africa of semi-arid land

## EXAMINER'S TIP: WRITING ABOUT MOVEMENT

The poem has a regular rhythm but the frequent enjambment, caesura and dashes break the regularity. For example, in the first line the pause comes before the end so that we follow the line on and read 'to rest / Uncoffined' (1, 2) and then pause again at the dash. These techniques emphasise the pathos of the drummer's situation, so the dignified movement of the poem becomes the missing tribute to Drummer Hodge and all young drummers who have died in war.

# Siegfried Sassoon: 'The Hero'

## SUMMARY

① The mother of a soldier receives a letter to say that he has died in combat.

② She consoles herself that he died bravely.

③ However, the visiting officer who has delivered the letter has lied to her.

④ As he leaves he thinks cynically to himself that Jack was a coward and no one but his mother cared about him.

## WHAT IS SPECIAL ABOUT THIS POEM?

A The poem explores **attitudes to war**, and its main theme is **hypocrisy**.

B It is written in three sestets with an energetic **rhythm** and tight rhyme scheme.

C The **language** is colloquial and ironic, creating a **cynical** tone.

## BROTHERLY LOVE

The officer who delivers the letter is described as a 'Brother Officer' (7). It is a deeply ironic description, for he shows no brotherly love towards Jack. He callously thinks of him as a 'cold-footed, useless swine' (13) and expresses no pity when Jack is 'Blown to small bits' (17). We sense there is no pity for the mother either, and the officer's 'gallant lies' (8) seem to have been told more from a need to follow army practice (as the Colonel's letter testifies) than to spare the mother's feelings. War, we might infer, has brutalised the officer. He also represents the broader position of those who cynically send young men to their deaths.

## THE MOTHER

The mother's attitude to war is summed up in lines 5 and 6. Pride in the fallen dead was common before the First World War, when war was regarded as a heroic enterprise. The mother is expressing these views. But she is ignorant of the realities of the trenches described in verse three and so is easily fooled by the officer's 'gallant lies' (8). Ironically, her son's death was the opposite of a 'glorious' (12) one.

## EXAMINER'S TIP: WRITING ABOUT THE RHYTHM AND RHYME

The iambic pentameter and regular rhyme patterns push the poem along, creating a rocking movement. In another kind of poem (a lyric poem, for example), these features might seem too marked. However, here they help to give an appropriate cadence to the everyday voices, and since the swaying rhythm is the opposite of the serious theme, the irony is reinforced. The poem would make a good performance poem, where the voices can be brought to life.

**★ GRADE BOOSTER**

Refer to the poem's colloquial language. For example, show how the officer's condescending attitude is revealed when he refers to the mother as 'the poor old dear' (8).

**CHECKPOINT 30**

What does the mother's comment about the Colonel tell you about her, and why is it ironic?

**GLOSSARY**

**trench** a deep and lengthy hole dug as a defence against gunfire

## Progress and revision check

REVISION ACTIVITY

① Why is the speaker so happy in 'The Sun Rising'?

.........................................................................................................

② Name two poems that discuss the nature and habits of a bird.

.........................................................................................................

③ Which poem is concerned with the death of a girl during war?

.........................................................................................................

④ Name a poem that depicts or discusses the birth of a child. Are then any others in the collection that do the same or similar?

.........................................................................................................

⑤ What does the speaker regret in 'My Grandmother?

.........................................................................................................

REVISION ACTIVITY

On a piece of paper write down answers to these questions:

● Why does the speaker in 'Cousin Kate' feel she has something more precious than Kate has at the end of the poem? Start: *The speaker feels that she has something more precious than Kate has at the end of the poem because … .*

● What argument does the speaker use when addressing young women in 'To the Virgins, To Make Much of Time'? Start: *The argument the speaker uses when addressing young women is that …*

## GRADE BOOSTER ★

In what way does the speaker explore love in Shakespeare's 'Sonnet 116'? Think about:

● what he says about faithfulness

● what he says about change

● the images that are used.

**For a C grade:** present your ideas clearly and suitably, using words from the question to guide your answer, and refer to specific examples from the poem.

**For an A grade:** ensure you give your own interpretation of the nature of the love described and how it is presented through the language in the poem, drawing on links and contrasts and referring to specific and relevant details in the text.

## Key themes

### RELATIONSHIPS

Love

The theme of love between men and women takes different forms in the collection, from the light and playful 'The Passionate Shepherd to His Love', to the celebratory 'Sonnet 43'. The latter, like 'Sonnet 116', explores the meaning of true love – something both suggest will outlast life. The witty poem 'The Sun Rising' is more complex than 'The Passionate Shepherd to His Love' and its intensity is as great as that of 'Sonnet 43'. But its concerns are with being in love, the kind of love that ignores the 'hours, days, months' (10) of the ordinary world. Time may not exist for such lovers in their own world, but they are not yet tested by time.

Other kinds of love are more scheming. The speaker in 'To His Coy Mistress' is focused on seduction, and while this is also true of the shepherd in 'The Passionate Shepherd to His Love', the effect of the witty, clever language in the former poem makes the speaker seem more calculating. In John Donne's 'The Flea', attempts at seduction become absurd as the flea that bites both the speaker and the lover is portrayed as a sacred temple in which the lovers' blood is mingled. The delicate poem 'Sonnet 18' is seductive in an entirely different way. The use of the second person, 'Thou' (you), makes the reader feel that they are being addressed directly. Since the image of beauty is an 'eternal summer' (9) it lives on, for as the speaker says, whenever the poem is read this beauty comes alive. The reader can therefore share in this pleasure.

'Valentine', a modern take on love, challenges romantic clichés. Instead of 'a red rose or a satin heart' (1), the lover is given an onion. It has the ability to produce tears and reminds us that love can be distressing as well as joyous.

Family and parent/child relationships

Family love, or the lack of it as depicted in 'My Grandmother', is also a theme of the collection. In this poem, the coldness of the relationship is acute. The speaker, looking back on her experience as a child, is filled with guilt and regret at not taking the opportunity to get to know her grandmother. When the grandmother dies, nothing remains, 'Only the new dust falling through the air' (24).

> **? DID YOU KNOW?**
>
> John Donne (1572–1631) is known for his complex and clever metaphors and conceits and is regarded as probably the most important of the metaphysical poets. As well as love poetry, he wrote songs, elegies, satires and sermons.

For the most part the relationships between parents and children in the collection are difficult, though also tender. They emphasise the anxieties of parenthood, and the son or daughter's need to assert their independence. Catrin, in the poem of the same name, is usually at odds with her mother, who is the speaker of the poem. The mother is both annoyed with and protective towards her daughter in the 'struggle' (15) that seems to dominate the relationship.

Conflict also occurs in Charles Causley's ballad 'What Has Happened to Lulu?' as it tells of Lulu's disappearance. The remaining child, who is insistent on asking the question, gets no satisfactory reply. The anguished mother, who throws a 'note on the fire' (11), gives us some clues, but for the most part keeps the secret close. And we never hear her words. They are reported indirectly through the child. The effect created is one of uncertainty. The reader is constantly asking what the relationship between Lulu and her mother was like and what *did* happen to her.

The ballad 'A Frosty Night' is similar in style and theme, but here it is the mother who asks the questions. She confronts her daughter about why she looks so ill, and what she has been doing. Again clues are given, but once more we are uncertain about what has happened. The mother is agitated, even over-excited. Is she fearful for her daughter, who like 'a ghost or angel' (23) has been dancing in frosty 'starlight' (24)? Is the supernatural at work? Or has she been with a lover? The effect of these ambiguities is to create a sense of foreboding as the tension between the mother and daughter mounts.

The moving elegy 'On My First Son' depicts the love of a father for his dead son, and 'Mid-term Break' reveals the strong bond within a family at the death of a small child. The principal theme in these poems is grief.

## REVISION ACTIVITY

Here are examples from the collection that share the theme of family or parent/child relationships. Are there any others?

- 'My Grandmother'

- 'Catrin'

- 'What Has Happened to Lulu?'

- 'On My First Son'

- 'Mid-term Break'

## Male/female relationships and the role of women

The relationships between men and women in the collection are varied. Some poems, such as Elizabeth Barrett Browning's 'Sonnet 43', depict harmony and also express emotions from the female point of view. This is a less common perspective, since most established poets were (and still are) men writing from a male standpoint. Another poem, 'The Willing Mistriss' by Aphra Behn, also expresses female emotions. However, it was written some two hundred years earlier than 'Sonnet 43'. More unusual still is its choice of subject: sexual desire. The speaker is a woman describing a woman's honest feelings. She 'return'd' (14) her lover 'many Kisses' (13) and gave in to passion. It is a marked challenge to the view that a woman should be virtuous and modest.

In some poems the woman is pursued by the man, where her depiction is much more conventional, and the effect for the modern reader is disturbing. In 'Whoso List to Hunt', she is a hunted deer, viewed as unobtainable prey, since she is owned by another man. There is a similar portrayal in 'The Beggar Woman' but the tone is very different. A gentleman is again out hunting, but this time the 'game' (4) (the woman) turns the tables on him.

The clearest demand for equality belongs to the speaker of 'A Woman to Her Lover', who requires fairness in marriage. The position of the 'vanquished' wife with the 'conqueror' (2) husband (which echoes the male/female position in 'Whoso List to Hunt') is not for her. She is happy to be his 'forever' (25) but only on equal terms. A wife who regrets her situation is the speaker in 'A Married State'. She has a serious message to give, but tells it in a lighter tone.

## REVISION ACTIVITY

Here are examples from the collection that share the theme of male/female relationships and the role of women. Are there any others?

- 'Sonnet 43'
- 'The Willing Mistriss'
- 'Whoso List to Hunt'
- 'The Beggar Woman'
- 'A Woman To Her Lover'
- 'A Married State'
- 'Twice Shy'

**DID YOU KNOW?**

The Irish poet Seamus Heaney (1939–) was awarded the Nobel Prize in Literature in 1995 and the T. S. Eliot Prize in 2006. His poetry is often concerned with the lives of ordinary people, small everyday events or observations of nature and with the exploration of the English language and its history.

Sometimes the relationships between men and women are touching. In Seamus Heaney's 'Twice Shy' both would-be lovers have been hurt in previous relationships. Embarking on a new one, they are hoping for the best, but are wary of dangers, as 'hawk and prey apart' (16).

## YOUTH AND AGE

Age is not treated with kindness in any of the poems. In 'Crabbed Age and Youth' (a poem written at a time when the average lifespan was thirty to forty years), it is a series of ills: shortness of breath, lameness, and 'full of care' (4). It is associated with the winter season when nothing grows, and is a symbol not only of personal decay but also of the continual movement towards death. In 'Sweet 18' age takes on a more sinister guise, as 'old Mother Time' (28), and wants to devour youth's 'warm flesh juices' (23). Even a close examination of age in 'Old Age Gets Up' tells us that 'having lived' (12) is an 'accident' (11), not a blessing. The only glimmer of hope is expressed in the determination of age to keep going, as it 'Pulls it pieces together' (20) to face another day.

Youth, on the other hand, is encouraged to make the most of its time, since 'That age is best which is the first' (9), as expressed in 'To the Virgins, To Make Much of Time'. Hurry, urges the speaker of 'To His Coy Mistress'. Time is short, so take your pleasures 'while the youthful hue / Sits on thy skin' (33–4). In 'Sweet 18', written over three hundred years later, the admiration for youth is still the same. It is beauty, 'innocence' and 'perfection' (9), much like the beauty represented in 'Sonnet 18'. Though youth is not actually mentioned in that sonnet, we assume it is a youthful beauty because it is associated with summer. The seasons often play a part in the depiction of age.

## POWER AND AMBITION

**EXAMINER'S TIP**

Remember that the main theme is the big idea running through the poem, such as 'power', but you need to ask further questions. What kind of power is it? Is it also to do with ambition, greed or conflict, for example?

One of the most blatant examples of personal power is the depiction of the Duke of Ferrara, in Robert Browning's 'My Last Duchess'. His power is inherited through the family line and his 'nine-hundred-years-old name' (33). His belief in his own superiority makes him demonic and he exerts control in a devastating way, bringing about the death of his wife. Ambitious for money as well as for power, he discusses the dowry his new wife will bring. We assume she knows nothing of his real self. At the end of the poem, the image of the god Neptune 'Taming a sea-horse' (55) is a metaphor for the oppression she will have to endure.

'Ozymandias' is an exploration of power and pride portrayed through the ruined statue of this 'king of kings' (10), whose power has long since gone. An absolute ruler in his day, he saw himself as immortal. But his ruined statue is all that remains and is an ironic reminder that even tyrants are powerless against time. The poem is a metaphor for all those in power who seek to oppress others.

The image of the hawk in 'Hawk Roosting' is another metaphor for power – and also ruthlessness. The bird is perfectly formed as a killing machine, for 'tearing off heads' (16). It has no moral sense by which it can be guided, so that regret, sorrow and guilt do not figure in its portrayal. This is a harsh portrait. And we can speculate that it is not only about a hawk. The images of its brutality and power are not far away from the images of war presented in 'Dulce et Decorum Est', for example, where men are maimed and killed. Perhaps we can read 'Hawk Roosting' as a comment on human power and ruthlessness and the way 'The allotment of death' (17) is meted out by humanity.

## HYPOCRISY AND PREJUDICE

The vanity of Thomas Hardy's preacher in the poem 'In Church' is a good example of hypocrisy. His concerns are to do with the effect he creates and the power he exerts on his congregation, rather than the content of his sermons. Perhaps the poem is also a broader commentary on the way that established religion can present a set of beliefs that are not always practised by its members. Similarly, Davies in 'Chapel Deacon' is preoccupied with worldly affairs – how his heifer will do in the local fair, for example – rather than heavenly ones. Of the war poems, most include hypocrisy in some form. In 'The Hero' it is revealed through the visiting officer's callous disregard for Jack.

Prejudice is a central theme of 'Refugee Blues', in which a whole race of people is discriminated against. In the poem 'You Will Be Hearing From Us Shortly', the small-scale prejudice of the interview room is depicted.

It is also an underlying theme in 'The Interrogation', since the border represents discrimination. Some groups of people can cross. Others cannot. In 'Displaced Person Looks at a Cage-bird', the outsider is a 'victim' (16) within society. Though he has somewhere to 'stay' (1), he is imprisoned in a way the bird is not, for as an outsider he has no real home and no access to some of the privileges the bird enjoys.

## REVISION ACTIVITY

Here are examples from the collection that share the theme of hypocrisy and/or prejudice. Are there any others?

- 'In Church'
- 'Chapel Deacon'
- 'The Hero'
- 'Refugee Blues'
- 'You Will Be Hearing From Us Shortly'
- 'The Interrogation'

**EXAMINER'S TIP**

Always keep a few questions in your head to help you stay focused in the assessment: *What are the key points I want to make? What is the evidence for these?* And most importantly: *How does the poet create effects?*

## CONFLICT

When we think of conflict, the war poems are the first to come to mind. Wilfred Owen's 'Dulce et Decorum Est' is one of the most disturbing. The images show how war breaks men in battle physically but also mentally, so that it haunts some as 'smothering dreams' (17) and makes us feel that it is an experience never forgotten. Similarly disturbing pictures, ghostly religious images of Christ, occur in 'The Conscript'. These are predictions. They show the results of the conflict to come. Though the mood is different in 'The Charge of the Light Brigade', where war is glorified, the poem nonetheless depicts large-scale conflict on the battlefield, partly through its movement and energy. In Thomas Hardy's 'The Man He Killed' conflict presents itself as a problem without an answer, a contradiction – how can you kill a man who might have been a friend had the circumstances been different?

However, conflict also exists in poems that explore other kinds of personal relationships, as we have seen in those involving a child and parent, such as 'Catrin', 'What Has Happened to Lulu?' and 'A Frosty Night'. 'Havisham' concerns the personal conflict within a character, springing from feelings of betrayal and hate so damaging that they all but destroy her as she makes 'sounds' that are 'not words' (9). Another of Duffy's poems, 'Human Interest', can be read in a similar way. Murder is clearly an example of conflict, but the murderer is also a conflicted person, struggling to justify his violence. Both characters are unable to cope with their grief.

## GRIEF

Conflict inevitably brings grief. In some of the war poems, grief as well as anger is present. In 'Dulce et Decorum Est', for example, the pause and the words 'My friend' (25) introduce a momentary note of calm, as though pausing in grief.

Grief dominates Owen's other poems in the collection, 'The Send-Off'. As men march towards the railway station that will take them to their death, the voice of the poem is heavy and the movement of the poem is slow. Though written in the First World War, the poem can be applied to all soldiers and those affected by war. 'MCMXIV' expresses grief for a lost culture that does not know its death is near. It is a lament for an England forever changed by the First World War.

Outside the war poems, grief is the main theme of poems such as 'Mid-Term Break'. The death of the speaker's brother punctures the lives of his family members. The last line, set apart, resonates, as we learn the age of the brother lying in 'the four foot box as in his cot' (20). Similarly, the grief the speaker feels in the elegy 'On My First Son' is profound, shown in the epitaph chosen for his lost child.

Family grief is also explored in 'Do Not Go Gentle Into That Good Night', but here it is expressed as a protest. The speaker urges his father to refuse death as that will be a way of celebrating life. He also finds it hard to accept that his father is dying, and the anger expressed and repeated in the word 'rage' seems close to tears. In Tony Harrison's 'Long Distance II', the speaker's father cannot come to terms with his wife's death, and behaves as if she is still with him. When the father dies, the speaker acts in a similar way, calling his father's 'disconnected number' (16) although he knows there will be no answer.

**KEY CONNECTION**

If you would like to read more of Wilfred Owen's poems about the First World War, the poems 'Futility' and 'Anthem for Doomed Youth' are two of the most well known and can be found in *The Collected Poems of Wilfred Owen*.

## Progress and revision check

REVISION ACTIVITY

① What kind of love is presented in 'The Passionate Shepherd to His Love'?

..................................................................................................................

② Name two poems in which conflict of different kinds occurs.

..................................................................................................................

③ Name a poem whose theme is hypocrisy.

..................................................................................................................

④ What do you think is the main theme of 'Ozymandias'?

..................................................................................................................

⑤ What are the themes in 'Sweet 18'?

..................................................................................................................

REVISION ACTIVITY

On a piece of paper, write down answers to these questions:

What is the theme in 'Valentine' and what is the speaker's attitude to it?
Start: *The theme in 'Valentine' is …The speaker's attitude to …*

Why does the speaker in 'A Refusal To Mourn the Death, by Fire, of a Child in London' not wish to mourn the child? Start: *The speaker does not wish to mourn the child because …*

## GRADE BOOSTER

How is the main theme of 'Dulce et Decorum Est' revealed in the last verse and how does the speaker employ this theme in the poem? Think about:

● what images are depicted

● what the last two lines tell us, why they are significant and who they are addressed to.

**For a C grade**: explain clearly what the theme is (using words from the question to guide your answer if you need to), and refer to specific examples from the poem to support your comments on the theme.

**For an A grade**: ensure that you show how the theme is revealed through the language in the poem, paying particular attention to the significance of the language in the last two lines, and the techniques used generally.

## Language

Here are some useful terms to know when writing about the collection, what they mean and examples from the poems.

| Literary Term | Means? | Example |
|---|---|---|
| caesura | a pause during a line of poetry to create an effect | Throughout the poem 'Human Interest', there are frequent pauses in the middle of lines creating a jarring, stop-start effect that suits the speaker's violent, disturbed character. |
| conceit | a complicated figure of speech involving comparison that is extended throughout a whole poem or series of lines; usually takes an idea or thing (such as the sun) and compares it with other things, in clever far-fetched ways | In the 'The Sun Rising' there are several comparisons with the sun. For example, the sun's beams, however strong, could be eclipsed by the speaker's wink, but that would mean he would lose sight of his lover, whose eyes could blind the sun. The conceit is used to convey the intense self-centred feelings lovers have. |
| connotation | an additional meaning attached to a word in specific circumstances (i.e. what it suggests or implies) | In 'A Frosty Night' the image of Alice as 'a ghost or angel' has connotations of death. |
| enjambment | when a line runs on into the next without pause, sometimes called a run-on line | In 'The Interrogation', line 11 runs on into line 12 and carries with it the sense that the refugees have been wearily standing all day gazing across the border while being questioned. |
| hyperbole | the use of exaggeration for effect | In 'To His Coy Mistress', the speaker says that if time was everlasting his love would grow 'Vaster than empires' (12). |

**EXAMINER'S TIP**

Try to remember the meaning of literary terms and distinguish between them. It is a good idea to note some down along with their names and definitions and some examples (to help you see the effect they have in the poem). Then try to memorise them.

## IMAGES FROM THE NATURAL WORLD

Images appeal to all the senses, but always to sight. They are the essential pictures that spring up in the mind as soon as we begin reading a poem.

In the traditional poems in the collection, poets often draw on nature, perhaps because the world around them was more rural than urban. In these poems, nature can be associated with pleasure, for example in 'The Willing Mistriss' where 'the Winds' (7) 'Kiss the yeilding Boughs' (8), or with escape as well as pleasure as in 'A Passionate Shepherd To His Love'. Similar images can also occur in modern poems. 'Leisure' praises the beauty of nature. The simile comparing 'Streams full of stars' with 'skies at night' (8) is a way of telling us that a life without time to appreciate nature is a 'poor' (13) one. In 'The Hunchback in the Park' the image of the woman, 'Straight as a young elm' (33) is perhaps a metaphor for the hunchback recreated, or a spirit of nature.

However, nature is not always soothing. In 'Hawk Roosting' the hawk, flawlessly created for survival, 'rehearse[s] perfect kills' in its 'sleep' (4). And in 'A Frosty Night' the 'chill night' (3), the shocked moon and the 'twittering' (15) birds have connotations of panic and death.

## IMAGES OF WAR

In several of the war poems the images of war are stark and unflinching. Their images flash before our eyes as we read, particularly in those of the gassed soldier in 'Dulce et Decorum Est and the 'thorn-crowned head' (13) and crucifixion in 'The Conscript'.

The images in 'The Charge of the Light Brigade', which are presented on a larger scale, also share this immediacy. Here it is do with a whole drama enacted through the poem's movement as well as the specific images of men, for instance lurching 'from the sabre-stroke' (35). Quieter poems such as 'Drummer Hodge' call up images of pity, as do the 'long uneven lines' (1), with their connotations of funerals, in the melancholy 'MCMXIV'.

Complex poems such as 'A Refusal To Mourn the Death, by Fire, of a Child in London' create a sense of nature continuing in the 'unmourning water' (22) of the Thames, despite the ravages of the Second World War. Brooke's poem 'The Soldier' also calls on nature, but in a very different way. It omits images of destruction and instead depicts a rural England forever part of 'some corner of a foreign field' (2).

## PORTRAITS

Imagery can also depict character, by describing what makes it distinctive. The image of Alice in 'A Frosty Night', as she dances in the snow with her eyes of 'frosted star-light' (25), suggests a young girl bewitched – or in love. The 'wild boys' (40) of 'The Hunchback in the Park' do as they please as they rush around roaring and 'Dodging the park keeper' (23).

Where a character addresses us directly we gain a sense of their nature through their voice (as in the dramatic monologue) but we also understand them through imagery. They are often striking and alarming characters. For instance, in 'Havisham' the speaker struggles with her feelings of humiliation and anger and we see her 'trembling' (7) as she stares at her distorted self in the mirror. In 'Porphyria's Lover' the image of Porphyria's corpse, 'the smiling rosy little head, / So glad' (52–3), as described through her murderer's eyes, tells us he would prefer her dead rather than alive – as the duke would in 'My Last Duchess'. The image of him pointing to her portrait, as though it is 'a wonder' (3) tells us he appreciates the portrait more than he did his wife.

**DID YOU KNOW?**

The sonnet remains one of the most durable forms in English poetry. It has lasted for over five hundred years and is frequently adapted by modern poets.

**EXAMINER'S TIP**

Try to remember the names of some traditional forms of poetry, examples of them and what they do. The dramatic monologue 'My Last Duchess' creates a strong sense of character, for example.

# THE LANGUAGE OF SPEECH

Everyday expressions help create character and mood. The use of slang and swearing produces an abrupt, harsh tone in 'Human Interest', to convey an image of a disturbed man. In 'Havisham' her 'Puce curses' (9) depict the speaker's mental torment.

Everyday language can also help to recreate the social position of the characters. In 'The Beggar Woman', a comment such as 'Mighty well, sir!' (34) tells us the beggar woman's social standing in relation to the squire. And even a single expression, such as 'sorry for my trouble' (10), immediately depicts the local people at the funeral in 'Mid-Term Break'.

Speech can also be used to convey formality – or to mock formality – for example, in the question 'Would you care / To defend their relevance' (8–9) in 'You Will Be Hearing From Us Shortly'. In 'My Last Duchess', the formal and archaic 'Will't please you sit ...' (5) places the setting of the poem in a past era.

In a poem such as 'Long Distance II' the language has a subduing effect. The style is low key, with little vivid imagery, and the words 'You couldn't just drop in' (5) create a conversational tone, so that the speaker seems to be addressing us directly. This intimacy helps to depict the grief the speaker feels at the loss of his father.

# Structure

## PATTERN AND PACE

The way the poem is presented on the page, its rhythm and movement and features that help to build patterns (such as repetition), create the poem's structure. In turn, these will relate to the meaning and ideas in the poem, its theme, and help to create the mood or tone. The bouncing rhythm, for example, in 'Base Details' clashes with the serious message, emphasising that the poem is a satire.

There are several examples of traditional, formal structures in the collection, such as sonnets (Sonnet 18), ballads ('What Has Happened to Lulu?') and elegies ('On My First Son'). These create different effects. For example, the strict pattern of the villanelle 'Do Not Go Gentle Into That Good Night', in which the two most important lines are repeated, builds to underline the poem's angry mood and the theme that death should be challenged.

Free verse also has its rhythms, even though they may not be regular. In 'Valentine', the movement is greatly affected by the pauses and spacing between lines that make the voice slow down. Where the pace changes the voice may run on lyrically, as it does in lines 4 and 5, creating the simile of the onion's layers of beauty.

# EXAMINER'S TIP: WRITING ABOUT HARMONY

Sometimes language and structure seem to be in harmony, for example in 'The Passionate Shepherd to His Love', where the repeating rhyme and the metre (iambic tetrameter) and quatrains give the poem a musical quality. This fits well with romantic love, the shepherd's songs and the birds' 'madrigals' (8).

**KEY CONNECTION**

The relationship between language and structure in 'Prayer Before Birth' can be seen in the grotesque images, the shortening lines (suggesting desperation) and the quickening anxious pace, particularly in the last verses. Read the poem closely and find more connections.

**EXAMINER'S TIP**

Sometimes language and structure seem to collide. Look back to the commentary on at 'Dulce et Decorum Est' on page 67 and note how the formal metre and rhyme scheme clash with the chaotic images of war.

**EXAMINER'S TIP**

Remember to refer to 'the speaker' (or if you prefer 'the poet') and avoid confusing the speaker with the poet. So for, example, 'The speaker/the poet describes his lover....' is fine, but not 'John Donne describes his lover ...'

## Progress and revision check

REVISION ACTIVITY

1 What image is used to depict the woman represented in 'Whoso List to Hunt'?

.............................................................................................................

2 In which poem will the lover be given a belt with 'coral clasps and amber studs'?

.............................................................................................................

3 In which poem does the imagery depict the landscape of 'The Bush' and the 'broad Karoo'?

.............................................................................................................

4 Which poem includes an epitaph?

.............................................................................................................

5 How would you describe the rhythm of 'The Charge of the Light Brigade'?

.............................................................................................................

REVISION ACTIVITY

On a piece of paper write down answers to these questions:

How does the language convey the interview situation in 'You Will be Hearing From Us Shortly'? Start: *The language conveys the interview situation in 'You Will be Hearing From Us Shortly' by …*

How does the pattern in the villanelle 'Do Not Go Gentle Into That Good Night' echo the poem's theme? Start: *The pattern in the villanelle 'Do Not Go Gentle Into That Good Night' echoes the poem's theme by …*

## GRADE BOOSTER

In what way is the character of Havisham, in the poem 'Havisham', portrayed through the imagery? Think about:

● Havisham's past

● how she feels

● what effect her feelings have on her.

**For a C grade:** make sure you discuss what the images mean (you could use words from the text to guide your answer) and how they help to build the portrait of Havisham, remembering to refer to specific examples.

**For an A grade:** make sure you show how the images are related, referring correctly to some of the literary techniques used. Also make sure you show how these help to build the portrait and what the effect on the reader might be.

# PART FIVE: GRADE BOOSTER

## Understanding the task

Your task is to link a play by Shakespeare with a selection of poems from the *WJEC Poetry Collection*. Your assignment is likely to be split into three parts:

- In the **first part,** you will write about the Shakespeare play and a key theme.

- In the **second part**, you will focus on one or two poems from the collection you have studied and how they relate to the theme. You will have to refer to other poems too.

- In the **final part**, you will link the poem/s and the Shakespeare play, comparing how they have approached the theme.

Here is an example of the sort of thing you might be asked to do:

> Many plays and poems are concerned with the relationship between parents and their children. Choose a **parent/child relationship** in a Shakespeare play you have studied and compare it with the way a **similar relationship** is presented in poetry. For example:
>
> - *Examine the way Shakespeare presents the relationship between Juliet and her father in* Romeo and Juliet.
>
> - *Explore how Ben Jonson presents his feelings for his son in 'On My First Son'. In your response, refer to other poems.*
>
> - *What is your response to the poems and play you have read? Make links between them.*

 **WRITE ABOUT MORE THAN ONE POEM**

When answering the **second part** of the assignment, make sure you refer to **several** poems on the theme you have been set. For example, begin by **focusing** on your main poem, e.g. 'On My First Son':

> 'On My First Son' is a moving elegy on the death of a child. The speaker's feelings of grief are mixed with those of guilt, because he fears that God is punishing him for loving his son so much and placing 'too much hope' (2) in him. So he questions fatherhood, only taking consolation in his son's escape from the 'world's and flesh's rage' (7) and the misery of growing old.

Then make a series of **further** points about this poem, and the way the idea has been explored. For example: 1) the impassioned voice conveys the deep grief the speaker feels; 2) the central image of the child as the speaker's 'best piece of poetry' (10); 3) how the poem moves from grief to despair to resignation.

Finally, link to **another** poem or poems (from the ones you have been set or given):

> In 'Catrin', a mother's mixed feelings towards her daughter are explored. The relationship has never been an easy one, as the daughter struggles to assert herself while the mother feels the demands and worries of being a parent. The image of skating 'In the dark' (29) depicts the apprehension the mother feels for her daughter as she grows, but also the excitement Catrin feels about her future.

And add any further relevant points. For example: 1) the image of childbirth shows the struggle between mother and daughter as they fight to be 'Separate' (16); 2) the struggle persists and neither mother nor daughter wins; 3) the bond between the two is shown in the metaphor, 'the red rope of love' (8), which also represents the umbilical cord.

## Planning your answer

**EXAMINER'S TIP**

The number of words and paragraphs you write will be determined by how long you take on this section of the assignment, but the key thing to remember is that whether you write 6, 8 or 10 paragraphs, you should make different points on the theme so that your argument is fully developed.

### ANNOTATE AND ORGANISE

When planning your response to the controlled assessment task, make **notes** on particular aspects of the poems you have studied, so that you have a **'ready reference'** for comparison, revision or planning purposes. For example, you might list ideas as shown below for the poem 'My Last Duchess':

| Key point/aspect | Evidence (quotation, reference to structure, etc.) | The effect this has or the idea conveyed |
|---|---|---|
| The poem is told by the Duke of Ferrara as a dramatic monologue. | 'and I choose Never to stoop' (42–3) | The voice conveys the Duke's pride and sense of superiority. |

### PLAN FOR PARAGRAPHS

Use paragraphs to plan your answer.

❶ The first paragraph should **introduce** the **argument** you wish to make.

❷ Then, jot down how the paragraphs that follow will **develop** this argument with **details**, **examples** and other possible **points of view**. Each paragraph is likely to deal with one point at a time.

❸ **Sum up** your argument in the last paragraph.

For example, for the following task:

**Question:** 'Compare how power is conveyed in the relationship between men and women in 'My Last Duchess' and refer to other poems from the collection.'

★ **GRADE BOOSTER**

It is vital that you plan your response to the controlled assessment task carefully, and that you then follow your plan, if you are to gain the higher grades.

Simple plan:
- *Paragraph 1:* Introduction
- *Paragraph 2:* First point – *explore attitudes to power and marriage in 'My Last Duchess' and make a point about the duke's domination and murder of his wife.*
- *Paragraph 3:* Second point – *further comment on attitudes in 'My Last Duchess' and the related point about how the duke values the portrait of his dead wife more than he valued her.*
- *Paragraph 4:* Third point – *explore attitudes to the same theme/issue in other poems from the collection.*
- *Paragraph 5:* Fourth point – *make a new point about attitudes to theme/issue in the other poem or poems.*
- *Paragraph 6:* Conclusion – *draw together what you want to say about the theme across the poems.*

# How to use quotations

One of the secrets of success in writing essays is to use quotations **effectively**. There are five basic principles:

❶ Put inverted commas at the beginning and end of the quotation.

❷ Write the quotation exactly as it appears in the original.

❸ Do not use a quotation that repeats what you have just written.

❹ Use the quotation so that it fits into your sentence.

❺ Only quote what is most useful.

 **USE QUOTATIONS TO DEVELOP YOUR ARGUMENT**

Quotations should be used to develop the line of thought in your essays. Your comment should not duplicate what is in your quotation. For example:

## GRADE D

## GRADE C

| (simply repeats the idea) | (makes a point and supports it with a relevant quotation) |
|---|---|
| The poet presents a happy picture of birds singing melodious songs. He says, 'Melodious birds sing madrigals.' | The poet presents a beautiful picture of nature in which the birds sing happily. The picture is one where 'Melodious birds sing madrigals'. |

However, the most sophisticated way of using the writer's words is to embed them into your sentence, and further develop the point:

## GRADE A

| (makes point, embeds quote and develops idea) |
|---|
| The poet's image of a natural world where 'Melodious birds sing madrigals' is an ideal one in which nature can provide all that is needed for a blissful, carefree life. Furthermore, 'madrigals' were sung as love poems so this suggests that love will also be part of this ideal world. |

When you use quotations in this way, you are demonstrating the ability to use text as evidence to support your ideas – not simply including words from the original to prove you have read it.

> **EXAMINER'S TIP**
>
> Try using a quotation to begin your response. You can use it as a launch-pad for your ideas, or as an idea you are going to argue against.

> **EXAMINER'S TIP**
>
> Where appropriate, refer to the language technique used and the effect it creates. For example, if you say 'this metaphor shows how …', or 'the effect of this metaphor is to emphasise to the reader …', this will get you much higher marks.

# Linking Shakespeare and poetry

In the controlled assessment, the **third part** of the task is about comparing the Shakespeare play you have read with poems from the *WJEC Poetry Collection*. Whether you are doing English or English Literature, the objectives you need to focus on are almost identical:

| Objectives | What does this mean? / Example |
|---|---|
| Write about the *similarities* and *differences* between the texts | Comment on the **general perspective or attitude** to the theme/issue in the play and the poetry and back it up with evidence. |
| | For example, you could comment on the way Macbeth begins as a respected soldier, and how with the murder of Duncan the king (Act 2 Scene 2) he becomes a ruthless killer in his quest for power. However, grim Fate also plays a part in Macbeth's ambition, in the guise of the witches, who convince Macbeth that he 'shalt be king hereafter' (Act 1 Scene 3). |
| | In a similar way, the hawk in 'Hawk Roosting' is also presented as a ruthless killer. However, there is no indication that he has lost his moral sense along the way. In his arrogance, he sees himself as all-powerful 'the path of my flight is direct' (18) – and he can choose 'to keep things like this' (24). |
| Write about the *different ways* the writers *achieve* their effects | Focus very specifically on the effect of **particular language devices** or decisions. |
| | For example, you could write about how in Act 1 Scene 7 Macbeth is troubled by his evil plotting against Duncan. He is fully aware that if he kills Duncan 'tears shall drown the wind,' a metaphor that shows the enormity of the crime and the misery that will follow. |
| | In 'Hawk Roosting', there is a similar awareness of reality. The hawk, although an untroubled character, suffers 'no falsifying dream' (2). This is a bold and direct image that convinces us that the hawk has no false impressions about itself. It will kill as it has to. |

## FINDING SIMILARITIES AND DIFFERENCES

On the surface there may not seem to be very much in common between a full-length play by Shakespeare and poems – some of which might have been written quite recently. But look **more closely**, and you will find you **can** make **links**:

 ## REMEMBER YOU WILL BE LOOKING AT A THEME OR IDEA

Themes or ideas such as Youth and Age or Conflict are universal concepts that many writers have written about, whether in plays or poetry. For example:

Driven by murderous ambition, Macbeth creates conflict until he is killed on the battlefield by Macduff. In the poem 'The Conscript' by Wilfrid Gibson, conflict is also a theme but here it is used to depict the horrors that await those who enlist and go to war.

 ## POEMS TELL STORIES AND HAVE CHARACTERS TOO

Thinking about what happens in a poem and the role of characters will help you make connections with Shakespeare's plays. For example:

In *The Tempest* Caliban is a slave whose mother was a witch and his father a sea monster, but he loves the natural beauty of the island on which he lives. In a similar way, the hunchback in 'The Hunchback in the Park' is an outcast who loves the park in which he spends his days.

 ## Shakespeare's language – similar to poetry?

All writers use language to tell their stories, reveal characters and explore themes. Shakespeare uses two different types of language – prose and poetry (verse) – in his plays, and some of the most famous passages from his plays are in verse.

In some cases the language in the poems is quite similar to Shakespeare's. At other times, it is quite different (even when tackling a similar theme).

For example, here is a similar use of imagery in a John Donne poem and a Shakespeare play:

| 'The Sun Rising' | *Romeo and Juliet* |
|---|---|
| 'is all states and all princes' refers to the perfection of his lover | 'This holy shrine' refers to Juliet's perfection |

However, here is Tony Harrison tackling the idea of loss but using language quite different from Shakespeare's:

| 'Long Distance II' | *Macbeth* |
|---|---|
| 'there's your name / and the disconnected number I still call' | 'I have words that would be howled out in the desert air' |

## Comparing and contrasting – how to make things clear

When writing this final part of your essay in which you link between poems and play, you will need to switch between texts and ideas, as you can see above. To do this, use **connectives** or other **linking words** or phrases.

There are several connectives that you can use to guide your argument and help to keep your writing clear. For example:

- 'Similarly', 'In the same way', *to make comparisons*
- 'Alternatively', 'On the one hand … on the other hand', *to make contrasts*
- 'However', 'Although', *to qualify or limit the meaning of a statement*
- 'In addition', 'As well as', *to add to a statement*
- 'Consequently', 'because', 'so', *to show cause and effect*

For example:

For Romeo, the lovesick hero of *Romeo and Juliet*, Juliet is 'This holy shrine' (Act 1 Scene 5), complete perfection. **Similarly**, the speaker in 'The Sun Rising' describes the perfection of his lover who 'is all states, and all princes' (21). **In addition**, both images are examples of hyperbole.

## Sitting the controlled assessment

When it comes to sitting the controlled assessment, follow these useful tips for success.

 **WHAT YOU ARE REQUIRED TO DO**

Make sure you are clear about:

- The **specific text** and **task** you are preparing (i.e. the Shakespeare play and the poems you've chosen).

- How **long** you have during the assessment period (i.e. 3–4 hours).

- How **much** you are expected or allowed to write (i.e. 2,000 words).

- **What** you are allowed to **take** into the controlled assessment, and what you can use (or not, as the case may be). You may be able to take in brief notes but not draft answers, so check with your teacher.

**EXAMINER'S TIP**

Remember, a poem may have more than one theme. For example, a poem's main theme might be 'love' but it might also include a theme about growing up. Try to identify themes other than the main one *where relevant*, and refer to evidence to show why it is a theme and how it relates to the main theme.

 **HOW YOU CAN PREPARE**

Once you know your task, topic and text/s you can:

- Make **notes** and **prepare** the **points**, **evidence**, **quotations**, etc. you are likely to use.

- Practise or draft **model answers**.

- Use these **York Notes** to hone your **skills** such as use of quotations, how to plan an answer and focus on what makes a **top grade**.

 **DURING THE CONTROLLED ASSESSMENT**

Remember:

- **Stick** to the topic and **task** you have been given.

- The allocated **time** is for **writing**, so make the most of it. It is double the time you might have in an exam, so you will be writing almost **twice as much** (or more) although you *may* also be writing on a larger number of poems.

- At the end of the controlled assessment follow your **teacher's instructions**. For example, make sure you have written your **name** clearly on all the pages you hand in.

# Improve your grade

It is useful to know the type of responses examiners are looking for when they award different grades. The following broad guidance should help you to improve your grade when responding to the task set.

## GRADE C

| What you need to show | What this means |
|---|---|
| **Personal sustained response** to task and text | You write enough! You don't run out of ideas after two paragraphs. |
| **Effective** use of textual **details** to support your explanations | You generally support what you say with evidence, e.g. *The grandmother in the poem of the same name is portrayed as loving 'the faded silks' and 'brass salvers' in her antique shop so much that she seemed to have 'no need of love' in relationships.* |
| **Explanation** of effects of writer's **use of language,** structure, form, etc. and **effect on readers** | You must write about the writer's use of these things. It's not enough simply to give a viewpoint. So, you might comment on the way a poet uses a final couplet to emphasise a point, or a powerful image to stress an idea, such as the metaphor of the 'wingèd chariot' representing time and how quickly it passes. |
| **Convey ideas clearly and appropriately** | What you say is relevant; if the task asks you to comment on how a setting is shown, that is what you write about. |

## GRADE A

| What you need to show *in addition* to the above | What this means |
|---|---|
| **Ability to speculate about the text and explore alternative responses** | You look beyond the obvious; you might question the idea of the mother's presence in the poem 'What Has Happened to Lulu?' What does her lack of clear answers to her child's repeated question suggest, and how do they add to the mysterious mood of the poem? |
| **Close analysis** and apt selection of **textual detail** | If you are looking at the writer's use of language you might focus very carefully on specific images that have subtle connotations of death in the poem 'Mid-Term Break'. For example, by selecting the quotation of the college 'bells knelling' in the second line you are able to show how the writer suggests not only the end of classes but also bells at a funeral. Flowers, such as the delicate 'Snowdrops', bring to mind the young boy's white face, while the 'poppy bruise' suggests blood. |
| **Confident** and **imaginative interpretation** | Your viewpoint is likely to convince the examiner. You show you have 'engaged' with the text, and come up with your own ideas. These may be based on what you have discussed in class or read about, but you have made your own decisions. |

# Annotated sample answers

This section will provide you with **extracts** from **two model answers**, one at **C grade** and one at **A grade**, to give you an idea of what is required to **achieve** at different levels.

> **Question:** Many plays and poems are concerned with the relationship between **adults and children**. Choose one relationship between an **adult and child** in the drama you have studied and compare it with a similar relationship in the poetry you have studied.
>
> *In the first section of the controlled assessment task, the student began by writing about Capulet and Juliet in* Romeo and Juliet *before dealing with the poems.*

## CANDIDATE 1

**Identifies what the poem is about but could say more about what the relationship is like**

**Uses a literary term and identifies an example**

**A good attempt to understand the nature of the relationship but the points need clarifying**

The poem 'Catrin' is about what the relationship is like between a mother and her daughter. The mother is the speaker. In the first verse there is a description of Catrin being born. The mother is remembering how hard it was and the umbilical cord comes into her mind. She calls it the 'tight red rope of love'. This is a metaphor for the umbilical cord. She also remembers writing over the walls with her words. I think this means that she screamed during childbirth. It's like quite an unusual image, but the words could be about screams of pain. Although she was in pain she loves her daughter because it says 'tender'.

There seems to be trouble between the mother and daughter because at the end of verse one the mother says quite clearly that the two of them wanted to be separate. It says they wanted 'to be two'. I think this tells us that the relationship between them is not easy but they are together because they are a mother and daughter and because of this they are torn both ways.

The poem is a free verse poem because the lines are of different lengths and it does not rhyme at the end of lines.

In the second verse Catrin is older. It says she has long brown hair. At the beginning of the verse the trouble between the mother and daughter still seems to be going on. Catrin wants to go skating and perhaps her mother doesn't want her to. It doesn't really say but it says 'defiant'. This tells us that Catrin is being rude or is saying what she wants. The image of the umbilical cord appears again. Perhaps it is reminding the mother of the way she and Catrin are linked and perhaps she doesn't want Catrin to go skating in case she gets hurt.

**Interprets the meaning of an image and hints at further meaning but does not develop the point**

**Uses the correct literary term to identify the form of the poem, but the definition is incorrect**

**Correct to raise the image again and makes a good attempt to explain it, but doesn't develop the explanation enough**

**Opens by comparing the two poems**

**Point supported by evidence**

**Correct to draw a link between the child's behaviour and the title, but could have taken this up later and expanded**

Like 'Catrin', the poem 'Follower' is also about a child and its parent but this time it is a father and son. The son is the speaker. When the son is small he follows his father around in the fields when his father is ploughing with horses, so it must have been a long time ago. The father has strong shoulders and he clicks at the horses to guide them. It says, 'His shoulders globed like a full sail strung'. He seems to be good at ploughing because it says he was an 'expert'. The little son follows him around and it reminds us of the way children are when they want to do what their parents do. It tells us that he fell down a lot in the mud and sometimes his father picked him up and gave him a piggyback.

I think the poem is called 'Follower' because the son follows his father around. In this way it is not like 'Catrin' because she seems not to get on with her mother very well.

At the end of the poem the son has grown up and the father is an old man and now he keeps falling. It is quite a sad picture cos it reminds us that we all grow old. The son doesn't seem to have the same feeling for his father as he did when he was small. In fact when it says 'will not go away', it suggests that his father gets on his nerves, which is not very nice.

*The student then went on to complete the task, linking the poems to Capulet and Juliet's relationship.*

**Identifies an important point but doesn't explore what it means in the poem**

**Correct to draw a contrast between the two poems but needs to expand**

**Recognises the shift in mood and the change in the image of the father, but could explore more thoroughly what this means for the relationship between the father and son**

**Overall comment:** The student has grasped the general meaning of the poems and has pointed to evidence to support the points made. A comparison has been attempted between the poems, but not in enough depth and sometimes the writing is a bit informal. The student has also attempted to look below the surface and explain the effects of language, but this needs further exploration. One other point: in using literary terms you need to be clear about what they mean. Free verse, for example, is a poem without a regular rhythm and does not follow any particular pattern, though it may contain some patterns such as rhyme.

**GRADE C**

CANDIDATE 2

**Question:** Many plays and poems are concerned with the relationship between **adults and children**. Choose one relationship between an **adult and child** in the drama you have studied and compare it with a similar relationship in the poetry you have studied.

*In the first section of the Controlled Assessment task, the student began by writing about Capulet and Juliet in* Romeo and Juliet *before dealing with the poems.*

**Identifies form**

**Identifies style and its effects**

**Quote embedded in sentence**

**Explores in depth the importance of a metaphor, showing how it can have opposite meanings and how it relates to the theme**

Written as a free verse poem, 'Catrin' describes the relationship between mother and daughter, as seen through the mother's eyes. From the first the relationship is a challenge for both of them and is depicted in a direct, energetic style, suited to the nature of their relationship. The pain of childbirth is conveyed in the image of the mother writing 'all over the walls with her words', her screams, but this is also a reference to her 'words' as a poet, another act of creation, apart from creating a child. The movements of childbirth are 'wild' but also 'tender', demonstrating that there is love as well as pain. The mother-daughter relationship is complex. The main image, 'the red rope of love', the umbilical cord, connects the child to the mother, but must be cut for the child to survive and become an individual. So it is a metaphor both for separation and for the bond between the parent and child. This conflict is at the root of the relationship and we can think of it as the main theme of the poem.

　The use of internal rhyme through its repetition also helps to give a suitable lilt to the lines and the reading voice, through words such as 'all' and 'wall' which, along with the soft alliteration of 'w' in 'wall', 'words', 'with' and 'wild', emphasises the love and affection felt towards the baby.

　In the second verse, we move forward as the mother and the older Catrin are placed opposite each other, still in conflict. Catrin rebelliously asserts herself as she asks whether she can continue to 'skate in the dark'. For her it is a metaphor for excitement. For the mother it represents Catrin's growing independence and her own anxiety about the unknown dangers that lie ahead in life for her daughter. The strain of responsibility and love shows as the 'red rope' tugs her heart.

　By contrast, the tone of 'Follower' is quieter. It traces the relationship between a grown son, the speaker of the poem, and his father, who is now an old man, revealing how their relationship has changed as the son has grown to adulthood and the father has aged.

**Shows the relationship between the poems' sound effects and language and the effect on the reader**

**Marks a shift in time**

Opens by contrasting the two poems and identifying the second poem's mood

**Identifies literary term and describes its effect**

**Contrasts the two poems**

**Contrasts the two poems**

The simile in the first verse, 'his shoulders globed like a full sail strung', shows the father in his prime as he ploughed a field, creating the image of a tough, muscular man with broad shoulders and his shirt billowing in the wind. The speaker as a young son adored his father and wanted to be as skilled as him. He wanted 'to close one eye' and 'stiffen' his 'arm' – the way his father judged the furrow to be ploughed. Instead he tripped awkwardly after him. He was like the title, the 'Follower'. This is very different from the depiction of Catrin. There is no suggestion that she wants to be like her mother.

Another difference between the poems is that 'Follower' has a regular rhythm and rhyme scheme that suggests the movement of the plough, 'Dipping and rising'. Enjambment is used to carry the last line of verse into the next creating the image, 'a single pluck / Of reins, the sweating team turned round'. It draws our attention to the way the father turns the horses and guides them up and down the field.

When the son reaches adulthood and the father ages, their positions seem to be reversed and a note of pathos is present in the image of the old man 'who keeps stumbling' after his son. It suggests he is now the follower and in the words 'will not go away' also an annoyance, just as the son was a 'nuisance' as a child. However, it could also suggest that the memory of his father and his skill persists, a skill that the son seems never to have achieved, and in this way he remains in his father's 'broad shadow'.

*The student then went on to complete the task, linking the poems to Capulet and Juliet's relationship.*

**Shows the relationship between the poem's sound effects and language**

**Could discuss in what ways the poems are similar, such as the undercurrent of conflict in 'Follower' and the more pronounced conflict in 'Catrin'**

**Overall comment:** An excellent answer to the question. The style is fluent and the analysis is detailed and well supported by evidence, including quotes embedded in sentences. The student has shown the relationships between the poems' language and structures and has drawn contrasts between the two poems. More could have been said in the second half on any similarities between the poems, for example an exploration of the types of conflict that exist between parent and child in both poems, but the overall quality is exceptionally high.

**GRADE A**

## Further controlled assessment-style tasks

1. Many plays and poems are concerned with the relationship between men and women.

- Choose one relationship between a man and woman in the drama you have studied and compare it with a similar relationship in the poetry you have studied.

2. Plays and poems sometimes involve the themes of power and ambition.

- Explore the different ways power and ambition are presented in the Shakespeare play and the poetry you have studied.

3. Love is a very common theme in poetry and drama.

- Explore the theme of love in the Shakespeare play you have studied and compare it with the way love is explored in the poetry you have studied.

4. Conflict is a theme in many plays and poetry. It maybe conflict between armies or countries or within personal relationships.

- Explore the theme of conflict in the Shakespeare play and the poetry you have studied.

5. Grief is a theme that is often explored in poetry and drama.

- Choose one example of grief from a Shakespeare play you have studied and compare it with the poetry you have studied.

## Literary terms

**alliteration** where the same sound is repeated in a stretch of language, usually at the beginning of words

**allusion** a reference in a work of literature to something outside the work, such as poetry, or biographical or historical detail

**ambiguity** when words or sentences have more than one meaning and it is not clear which is the true interpretation

**apostrophe** a poem in which the speaker talks to someone or something not present

**archaic** belonging to earlier or ancient times

**aside** in theatre, an actor's remark spoken to the audience rather than to other characters

**assonance** when the same vowel sound appears in the same place in a series of words

**aubade** a poem or song about lovers separating at dawn

**ballad** a traditional story written in rhyme with four lines to a verse

**blues** music that originated in African American communities, that has influenced a range of other musical forms in the twentieth and twenty-first centuries

**cadence** the recurring rise and fall of the rhythms of speech; it can also refer to a rhythm that comes at the close of a line or poem

**caesura** a pause during a line of poetry

**call and response** an unprompted verbal interaction between a speaker and listener (for example, when a blues song is sung)

**cliché** an overused word or phrase that has lost its original power

**closed couplet** a couplet in which the main thought or image is expressed in the two lines

**colloquial** the everyday speech used by people in ordinary situations

**conceit** a complicated figure of speech involving comparison that is extended throughout a whole poem or series of lines. It usually takes an idea or thing and compares it with other things, in clever far-fetched ways.

**connotation** an additional meaning attached to a word in specific circumstances, i.e. what it suggests or implies

**couplet** two lines of poetry that are paired. See also closed couplet and rhyming couplet

**courtly love** noble love expressing desire and admiration, popular during the Middle Ages

**double meaning** a word or expression having two (or more) meanings, sometimes called a pun

**double negative** grammatically, the incorrect use of two negatives in a clause or sentence. It can sometimes have the effect of creating the opposite meaning of what was intended, e.g. *He never went nowhere*

**dramatic monologue** a poetic form in which a single voice addresses the reader, creating a strong sense of character

**elegy** a poem lamenting a death

**ellipsis** the omission of words in a line or sentence

**end-rhyme** rhyme at the end of lines of poetry

**enjambment** in poetry, when a line runs on into the next without pause, so carrying the thought with it. Sometimes called run-on line

**epitaph** an inscription on a grave, or writing suitable for the purpose

**extended metaphor** in poetry, a metaphor that continues some aspect of the image; it may continue into the next line or throughout the poem

**folk song** a traditional song of the people

**foot** a unit of rhythm

**free verse** a form of poetry; verses without a regular rhythm or pattern, though they may contain some patterns such as rhyme.

**gothic** gloomy and horrifying

**half-rhyme** where the rhyme at the end of a line has the same consonants but not the same vowel sound, so not quite a full rhyme, e.g. pet/pat

**hyperbole** the use of exaggeration for effect

**iamb** a weak stress followed by a strong stress;

**iambic pentameter** see iamb; pentameter: a line of poetry consisting of five iambic feet

**iambic tetrameter** see iamb; tetrameter: a line of poetry consisting of four iambic feet

**iambic trimeter** see iamb; trimeter: a line of poetry consisting of three iambic feet

**idiom** an everyday expression or a common saying in a language

**idyll** a short poem describing a picturesque scene or event in rural life

**imagery** descriptive language that uses images to make actions, objects and characters more vivid in the reader's mind

**imperative** expressing a command, e.g. Come in!

**irony** deliberately saying one thing when you mean another, usually in a humorous or sarcastic way

**lyric** a poem expressing the speaker's personal thoughts and feelings

**jingo** a popular patriotic song

**juxtaposition** contrasting ideas placed together

**madrigal** a song or poem set to music, popular in the sixteenth and seventeenth centuries and earlier

**metaphor** when one thing is used to describe another to create a striking or unusual image

**metaphysical poetry** the name given to poetry written by a group of seventeenth-century poets who were concerned with analysis rather than feeling, and used complex and sometimes exaggerated imagery and clever, bold ideas

**metre** the pattern of stressed and unstressed syllables in a line of verse

**motif** a repeated theme or idea

**narrative poem** a poem that tells a story

**octave** a verse of eight lines, usually in iambic pentameter; the first eight lines of a sonnet

**omniscient** a speaker's voice that sees and knows everything that happens

**pastiche** a poem or work of art that mimics another poem or style

**parody** a literary work that mimics another work or style in order to ridicule it

**pastoral** a poem with a rural setting depicted in an idealised way

**pathos** a point in a poem or work of art where strong feelings of sadness are evoked

**performance poem** a poem suited to being performed

**personification** when things or ideas are treated as if they were people, with human attributes and feelings

**Petrarchan sonnet** a sonnet that has an *abba abba* rhyme scheme followed by a sestet *cdcdcd*, though the pattern may vary slightly

**projective verse** an idea of the poet and essayist Charles Olson describing free verse in which the reader is encouraged to read the poem in the way the poet wrote it and wants the reader to read it. So the reader would gather pace or slow down according to the way the poem is set out

**prose** spoken or written language as generally used, e.g. continuous writing as in a novel or story

**quatrain** four lines of verse; can stand alone or be a repeating form in a poem

**quintain** five lines of verse; can stand alone or be a repeating form in a poem

**refrain** repeated lines or groups of words that convey the same meaning

**repetition** repeated words or patterns in a poem

**requiem** in the Christian religion, prayers and music for the souls of the dead

**rhetoric** the skill of persuasive speaking or writing; a rhetorical question is one that expects no answer, often used for effect

**rhyme scheme** the pattern of rhyme in a poem

**rhyming couplet** two lines of poetry, usually the same length, that rhyme

**satire** a type of literature in which topical issues are ridiculed

**sestet** a verse of six lines

**setting** the place and time in which a work of art is set

**Shakespearean sonnet** a sonnet that has an *abab cdcd efef gg* rhyme scheme

**sibilant** a hissing sound in speech made, for example, with an 's' or 'sh'

**simile** when one thing is compared directly to another using the word 'like' or 'as'

**sonnet** a fourteen-line verse with a rhyming couplet at the end

**stanza** a group or pattern of lines forming a verse

**stream of consciousness** writing in which the speaker's or character's thought processes follow in a loose, dreamlike way as ideas flow into each other

**surreal** strange and dreamlike

**symbol** something that represents something else, usually with meanings that are widely known, e.g. a dove as the symbol of peace

**talking blues** blues in which the lyrics are close to speech, the melody loose, and the rhythm strict

**tercet** a verse of three lines

**terza rima** a verse of three lines with the rhyme scheme *aba bcb cdc* and so on

**theme** an idea running through a work of literature or art

**tone** the mood created by an artistic work

**unstressed syllable** a syllable with a weak stress

**vernacular** language or dialect spoken in a region

**villanelle** a poem of six verses; the first five verses are three lines and the final verse is four; the first and last line of the first verse are repeated in turn as the last line of the next four verses and then become the last two lines in the poem

**voice** the speaker or narrator of a poem or a work of fiction. This persona is created in the reader's mind, though sometimes it can seem close to the poet's or writer's own voice

**volta** the turn or shift in a sonnet (usually after the octave), when a second idea or mood is introduced

# Checkpoint answers

**Checkpoint 1:** Andrew Marvell. (Shakespeare has aspects of the metaphysical in his work, but is not usually thought of as a metaphysical poet.)

**Checkpoint 2:** A 'childhood's faith' suggests a simple, straightforward and trusting kind of love.

**Checkpoint 3:** The 'red rose', the 'cute card' and the 'kissogram' are other symbols of love.

**Checkpoint 4:** The use of dialogue makes us feel the characters' presence.

**Checkpoint 5:** 'The Flea' was written when Donne was young, and he shows a certain disdain for religion. Holy Sonnet 17 was written when he was much older and he had become a priest in the Anglican church.

**Checkpoint 6:**
Answer: 'shoulders', 'shafts'; 'sail strung', 'strained'; 'father', 'full', 'furrow'.

**Checkpoint 7:** The words refer to Ben Jonson's poem 'My First Son', in which he describes his son as 'his best piece of poetry'.

**Checkpoint 8:** It is difficult to find much hope in this poem, since it reflects feelings of devastation during a war. The voice asks to be heard and protected. Perhaps this is a sign of hope for future generations.

**Checkpoint 9:** In verse two when the grandmother asks her granddaughter to go out with her, and this might be a sign of the need for love.

**Checkpoint 10:** The restricted view from the window is the same view everyday, suggesting that life is also restricted.

**Checkpoint 11:**
Answer: 'ivy resting her lameness' or 'old Mother Time'.

**Checkpoint 12:** We can assume Porphyria's lover is thinking about how to kill her.

**Checkpoint 13:** The speaker seems unable to grasp the reality that he is a murderer when he says 'I wouldn't harm a fly, no joke'.

**Checkpoint 14:** The focus in the final lines is on the duke's tyrannical nature and disturbing self-interest.

**Checkpoint 15:** The poet would appear to be critical of the monarchy since the poem describes a ruthless king. On the other hand, he values art since he praises the sculptor's work in creating the statue of Ozymandias.

**Checkpoint 16:** Similes: 'a small wind tugged at their clothing like a dog' (6) suggests a pestering, unkind, wind and 'the city / Enormous and still like a great sleeping seal' (11–12) suggests a lumpen, motionless, wet mass – wet because it links to 'rain' in line 11.

**Checkpoint 17:** These words refer to the way in which everything around you including time seems distorted when you are in love.

**Checkpoint 18:** This image suggests that the mothers in the poem who live on the estate lead a dreary domestic life.

**Checkpoint 19:** 'Give me a male corpse for a long slow honeymoon' suggests that Havisham hates all men.

**Checkpoint 20:** These descriptions suggest the nervousness felt by the couple when they meet.

**Checkpoint 21:** The word 'astray' refers to the squire having chosen to lose his way in the wood and also to his having lost his way in a moral sense, because he intends to take advantage of the beggar woman.

**Checkpoint 22:** The repeated words emphasise a feeling of boredom and weariness.

**Checkpoint 23:** 'Base' can mean immoral, or the centre of operations such as an army camp. 'Details' also has several meanings: a list of facts, a small party of troops with a special duty (detail), or full information on something.

**Checkpoint 24:** The word suggests that the troubadour crows like a cockerel, and is boastful. However, the word also has associations with 'capon' (1), a cockerel that is impotent.

**Checkpoint 25:** As the poem is a dramatic monologue it could be staged so that the interviewer addresses the audience or an imaginary interviewee. Only simple props such as a table and chairs would be necessary and the interviewer's additional comments could be delivered as asides.

**Checkpoint 26:** The consul says, 'If you've go no passport you're officially dead'. This means that without a passport the refugee has no identity and therefore officially does not exist.

**Checkpoint 27:** The exclamation marks give the voice greater emphasis and provide drama while the dashes and ellipsis create a pause, slowing down the reading voice.

**Checkpoint 28:** He is standing with his arms outstretched and his head down for his medical check. This reflects the image of Christ on the cross.

**Checkpoint 29:** Answer: 'Someone had blundered', meaning that those in charge were to blame.

**Checkpoint 30:** Her comment suggests that she respects the colonel's authority because of his position, and also that she believes he cared about her son. It is ironic because the colonel has clearly not told her the truth about Jack's death.